No Local

Why Small-Scale Alternatives
Won't Change The World

No Local

Why Small-Scale Alternatives
Won't Change The World

Greg Sharzer

Winchester, UK
Washington, USA

First published by Zero Books, 2012
Zero Books is an imprint of John Hunt Publishing Ltd., Laurel House, Station Approach,
Alresford, Hants, SO24 9JH, UK
office1@o-books.net
www.o-books.com

For distributor details and how to order please visit the 'Ordering' section on our website.

ISBN: 978 1 84694 671 4

A CIP catalogue record for this book is available from the British Library.

Design: Stuart Davies

Printed in the UK by CPI Antony Rowe
Printed in the USA by Offset Paperback Mfrs, Inc

We operate a distinctive and ethical publishing philosophy in all
areas of our business, from our global network of authors to
production and worldwide distribution.

CONTENTS

This book is dedicated to Punita, whose determination has inspired my own.

Preface

Some time ago, I was talking with a nutritionist friend about how expensive and time–consuming it is to be poor. You have to chase low–wage jobs, live in poor–quality housing and endure the daily stress of trying to afford the essentials. Government, which used to provide a social safety net, doesn't help much. Warming to the topic, I added, "They don't even provide spaces for community gardens."

My friend replied, "Why should poor people have to grow their own food?"

I had never considered this before. When you're poor, time and energy aren't the only things to go: the first is dignity, as you're forced to scrape by on less. Is there anything noble in adding yet another burden of work? Yet dozens of boosters claim the exact opposite: growing, making and doing it yourself is supposed to be liberating. This book groups all of them together under the label of localism, because they have a common thread: the belief that small, ethical alternatives can build quality communities, outcompete big corporations and maybe even transform capitalism.

Some of this is left–wing, but the Right shares that vision as well. For example, the UK's Department of Community and Local Government homepage invokes "Localism, localism, localism" and has created a localism bill that devolves power to communities, claiming that a "radical localist vision is turning Whitehall on its head by decentralizing central government and giving power to the people." When anarchists and Tories both claim local spaces for their own, we need to clarify exactly what localism is.

Localism begins with the principle that when things grow too big, communities and collective values suffer. Concentrating economic and political power creates inequality. Owners of big factories who live far away don't care about workers and the environment. In response, localism says we can change how we act within capitalism. If consumers don't like a commodity, they can demonstrate their commitment to a better one: for example, choosing to buy a Fair Trade cup of coffee. Support ethical, small–scale businesses and little by little the excesses of economic growth will disappear. More radical localists say that power and size are integral to capitalism and the system needs to change; to do so, we can work together to make and distribute ethical products outside the market. Community gardening, farmers' markets and biofuel movements will change the entrenched power of agribusiness. Foodies and locavores unite: you have nothing to lose but your fast food chains.

However, while small–scale alternatives can survive and occasionally flourish, they won't build a new, equitable society. Their prospects are severely limited by the power of capital. The problem with localism is not its anti–corporate politics, but that those politics don't go far enough. It sees the effects of unbridled competition but not its cause.

This is not a book about the successes and challenges of a particular community garden or biodiesel scheme. That research is important, but it's already been done: there are plenty of detailed empirical surveys of local projects and their participants. They usually end with the hope that people will take the example and try it elsewhere, implying that local projects can be spread throughout the economy. But if localists had a greater under-standing of how capitalism works, they might not be localists. That's why *No Local* is largely a theoretical book. Although it examines plenty of localist projects, its purpose is to provide what they lack: a critical understanding of the internal drives of capitalism and how they limit the potential for small–scale alter-natives.

Karl Marx showed how capitalists must do everything possible to sell their commodities at the lowest price. That means lowering wages and not paying for environmental costs. Firms do so not because they're evil but because they have to grow. If they don't, they'll be forced into bankruptcy.

OK, some might say, localism might not change everything. But at least it's doing something. And in fact, the whole point of being a locavore is that it's *not* trying to bring down global systems (and who's ever done that?) Localism makes small, incremental changes within our reach. If the net result is that the world is fairer and greener, so much the better; if it's not, no one gets hurt, and maybe we get a few good crops of tomatoes out of it. In that sense, localism is a kind of pluralism: you build your big social movements over there, we'll set up our farmers' market over here, and sooner or later the two will add up. We don't have to choose between the two.

If you want to create healthy food for yourself or trade crafts, that's great. Making something yourself, whether it's a painting, a bicycle or a carrot, is a way to feel you've left a mark in a world where everything's bought and sold. If growing your own vegetables makes you feel better and helps you meet your neighbors, then you should do it. Moreover, participating in a local DIY project can provide the strength and tools for community activism. Inspiration and political imagination are highly personal and subjective things, and no one can predict what inspires a critical understanding of society and how to change it.

But if the goal is stop ecological degradation and runaway growth, then the stakes are higher, and localists need to ask whether small projects will create long-term change. In practice, building those alternatives takes a lot of time and energy; projects can become self-justifying, not the means to build broad movements for social change. That's why this book argues that hidden beneath localism's DIY attitude is a deep pessimism: it assumes we can't make large-scale, collective social change. Those with the correct ideas can carve a niche outside the system, but for most people, the machinery of capitalism will continue to be oiled with the blood of its workers.

Political economy deals with big, abstract laws, which can imply there's nothing for us to do but lie down before the steam-roller of economics. Given this logic, it's tempting to focus on how people are making a better world right now. The problem is that even if we ignore capitalism, it won't ignore us. If we under-stand how the capitalist system grows and lurches from crisis to crisis, we can understand our own possibilities for action.

If small–scale, local changes won't change the system, what can we do? Lots: if we understand how capitalism works, we can act to transform it. This is the project of *No Local*: to sketch the outline of capitalism and apply it to localist plans for change. Chapter One shows how Marx anticipated localism, debating the political economists of his day about how economies work. Classical economists said capital was a collection of tradeable objects. Everyone comes to market to sell products, either commodities or their own labor. The market is neutral, there's no power involved, and it follows that entire economies can be re–organized according to our personal preferences. Marx, on the other hand, defined capital as the power to exploit. Capitalists own factories, fields and offices, collectively called the means of production. The owners have to grow their firms or die. Workers, on the other hand, own nothing but their capacity to work, which they sell on the labor market. They have to work or die. Capital tries to make the cheapest possible commodities, while workers try to stretch their wages by buying cheaper goods. Smaller firms are squeezed between both forces.

Chapter Two looks at how localists have applied these ideas, in both pro– and anti–market ways. Pro–market localists believe small business is always more ethical and environmentally friendly, keeping local money in the community. But this isn't always true: due to their size, small businesses often cut corners and don't treat their workers better. Anti–market localists don't share these illusions, but they still believe building small projects can transform capitalism, creating decentralized economies with simple technologies and alternative currencies. In both cases, capital places strict limits on the ability of small businesses or ethical, social alternatives to change it. To overcome these limits, localists look to ethical consumers to pay more for local products; however, consumers don't have the power to change capitalism.

Chapter Three examines food politics, which raise important questions about the quality of food and the sustainability of large-scale agriculture. Localism suggests urban agriculture (UA) can overcome malnutrition and promote ethical production. However, capital's drive to expand appears on the land too, in the form of rent, which means UA must generate higher profits than any other potential land use. Pro-market UA can sometimes find market niches; anti-market UA faces an uphill battle. In both cases, existing high rents in cities mean it's far more likely that land will be put to more profitable uses than community gardens.

Chapter Four suggests that localism's values of morality, community and voluntary effort appeal to the class of professionals and managers who make up the middle strata of society. Full of nostalgia for a bygone era, these people create visions of community based on small-scale entrepreneurship, or try to transcend capitalism by appealing to utopias. When small, incremental changes don't add up, localists can end up blaming consumers who buy the wrong things. By creating a sense of elitism based on consumer choice, localism pushes out other, more collective kinds of politics with more potential to change society.

Chapter Five suggests political alternatives to localism. Neoliberalism, the ideology of market deregulation, has used localism to transfer social costs onto the working class. Without understanding capitalist laws of motion, localism can become a tool to implement pro–market reforms. This even appears in anti–market theories like postcapitalism which, in an effort to avoid capitalism, ends up reconciling with it. We don't need to live the future society today; rather, Marxism provides a way to build counter–power within capitalism, creating social movements to transform it.

Since the bank bailouts of 2008, governments have said that we have to pay for the crisis. The $20 trillion given to financial institutions worldwide has been matched by the scale of cutbacks to social services. In this context, trying to make small–scale change to a system intent on stealing from as many people as possible makes even less sense. The corporate class is acting globally; so should we. The 2011 uprisings in the Middle East have not only given voice to the democratic ideals of entire peoples: they've put mass struggle back on the agenda. We have concrete evidence that collective resistance can topple dictators. If you agree that capitalism degrades our communities and the earth, what comes next? This book argues that if we understand how capitalism works, we can do more than tinker around the edges: we can build anti–capitalist movements to create a world where human need, and not growth, is the goal of development.

No writing project is individual, no matter how it may feel at the time, and this book comes out of conversations with and the support of many people. There are too many to list, but in particular I'd like to thank David McNally, who provided invaluable critical feedback for this project. Greg Albo introduced me to classical political economy and clarified the circuit of capital. Alan Sears and Jamie Gough contributed much–needed feedback on the initial chapters. The friendship and support of Alexi, Andrew, Anya, Chris, David, Keith, Lesley, Rashmee, Sabine, Shirley, Veronique and many others have helped me immensely. My successes are in large measure due to these people; all errors and obfuscations are, of course, my responsibility.

Chapter One

Twenty First Century Capitalism, Nineteenth Century Economics

What is the local?

No one's entirely sure. In the Hundred Mile Diet, Alisa Smith and James MacKinnon define it as the local watershed, but all watersheds can't grow the same kind of crops or provide the same raw materials. Likewise, every localist praises local community, but is a community an entire town or just a neighborhood? What if the owner of the local business lives in another community? Some localists say that you should try to purchase locally–made goods when possible. But commodities don't come into the world fully formed: they have to be made, processed, distributed and sold, in a process involves commodities and labor from across the globe. If these goods are local because of who's selling them, but use globally–assembled vehicles, roads, fuel, packaging and credit systems for distribution, how does this make a local economy?

The point of raising all these questions is not to answer them but to point out that they are largely *unanswerable*. The local, by definition, is a space distinct from regional, national and international spaces. The closer one looks, the more complex and varied local spaces become. Capitalism, which brings local spaces into the global market, complicates the situation still further. Local spaces are no longer just sites where people live or work, but *relational*: capital and workers flow through localities on their way to other localities or become fixed points of globe–straddling production and finance networks. For the purposes of this book, the local is simply one node of those vast networks, as Marx pointed out in *The Communist Manifesto*: "In place of the old local and national seclusion and self–sufficiency, we have inter-course in every direction, universal interdependence of nations." Not everyone is pleased with this state of affairs.

What is localism?

Localism begins with a criticism of size: factories, governments or bureaucracies have grown too big, and that causes human misery and environmental catastrophe.[1] There is plenty of evidence for that destruction. Finite supplies of oil and water are being depleted: for example, 85 percent of California water is used for agriculture, draining entire rivers, while fossil fuels are used for fertilizers and transportation. Food production and transport uses up 20 percent of all US fuel. As production grows, so does ownership: four companies control 81 percent of US beef production; another four control over 70 percent of fluid milk sales in US, while four more control 85 percent of global coffee roasting. Five companies control 75 percent of the global seed market in vegetables.

For localism, the effect of all this growth goes beyond the economy: it kills our souls as well. Intelligence, happiness and peace disappear in the quest for wealth. Personal alienation comes from the depressing monocultures of urbanization, indus-trialism, globalization, science and technology. The richer a society gets the more unsustainable and miserable it becomes.

This concept has roots in classical economics. Adam Smith, Thomas Malthus, David Ricardo and others thought economies would exhaust their natural resources. Surplus production would be used up paying for basic needs and rent, creating steady–state economies with no profit or growth. The modern environmental movement turned this into a goal: in his seminal 1973 book *Small is Beautiful*, Eric Schumacher denounced mainstream or neoclassical economics for promoting growth for growth's sake. He and other localists recognized that economies of scale transform industry. Schumacher saw the quest for low prices, low wages and lax safety standards as a consequence of how mainstream economics favors more, rather than better goods, equating corporate with social good and ignoring how private greed threatens the whole planet. The 1987 UN report *Our Common Future* summarized the perspective best, when it said production should prioritize people's needs and the ecosystem instead of technology and unlimited development, calling for wealth redistribution, slower population growth and restricted resource use. Arne Naess, the founder of deep ecology, called for socialists and environmentalists to unite for equality and against hierarchy and market excesses.

For the past 20 years, neoliberal ideologues have proclaimed the end of history. Neoliberalism is a set of ideas that promotes market rule: get big government out of the way, and the free play of competitive market forces will make everyone rich. Anyone who dares to suggest society should be organized to meet human need is ridiculed or ignored. Localism deserves praise for refusing to abandon a humanist vision of the future, and for suggesting we're not completely powerless against neoliberalism. But localism remains confused about what the capitalist economy is, and this hampers its ability to pose alternatives. To understand what makes capitalism unique, and why individual consumers and small business owners count for very little, we have to understand where market power comes from.

Localism and value
Although localists themselves may not know it, their ideas were widely held in the nineteenth century when economists debated how to respond to the vast changes taking place in newly industrializing, capitalist society. If they could define the source of wealth, they could tell governments how to make their economies grow.[2] Previously, Adam Smith was the first major economist to create a labor theory of value: the value of goods came from the labor put into them. But some goods take more

work than others, and Smith couldn't figure out how to decide how much that labor was worth. Moreover, capital and land also appeared to be sources of wealth. In the end he decided value came from labor, capital and rent from the land.

David Ricardo dealt with both objections. First, he said the value of goods could be counted in units of unskilled labor. Add them up, and you could figure out the price of skilled labor and any commodity made from it. Second, he thought capital and rent were products of *past* labor. For example, the value of stockings included far more than assembling the final product. It included growing the cotton, transporting it to the mill, making tools and so on. At each point, it was workers' labor that added wealth to the process.

The implications were radical: labor created all wealth, and capitalists exercised despotic control over production. However, Ricardo was a stalwart defender of the capitalist order. He maintained that capital was a thing, equating it with capital goods, tools and machinery that smart entrepreneurs could accumulate, driving economic growth. This was capitalism perfected: human history led up to it and then stopped.

Marx took up where Ricardo left off.[3] He found that goods have two sides. First, they have a use–value: what an object is worth according to its concrete, material qualities. The use–value of a computer is that it lets you write and correct documents, for example. But objects made for sale have a very different, second quality: their exchange–value, what an object is worth according to the market. If the customers are too poor, they can't afford to purchase them, the capitalist doesn't get her exchange–value and the computer remains useless. This is why Marx said exchange–value colonizes use–value: an object might start off with a set of physical, material uses, but the need to make a profit will blot them out.

Labor itself is a commodity, and under capitalism it takes the form of wage work. It's the only commodity that creates *more* value than it takes to make it. If a worker works eight hours a day, she gets paid the equivalent of four. In other words, she generates more wealth than she earns. The gap between her wages and that extra wealth is surplus value. Her wages pay for her maintenance: the capitalist pockets the rest.

Note that Marx wasn't complaining about low or unfair wages, but about the wage relationship as a whole. Even if workers received the full value of what they produced, they'd still be paid in capital taken from other workers. This undercuts the entire concept of fair capitalism. For example, usury, buying low and selling high, doesn't create any new wealth, it just redistributes existing value to the retailer who's overcharging. The theft of value comes *before* the market. As Marx put it, "the whole thing still remains the age–old activity of the conqueror, who buys commodities from the conquered with the money he has stolen from them." It's hidden: by contracting for a wage, the worker gets paid exactly what the capitalist says that time is worth.

Put differently, capital is a *social relation*, not a gold bar or a piece of equipment. It's the ability to capture and use the labor power of others. The only way capitalists get it is by denying ownership to everyone else. Marx saw it first in the enclosures of seventeenth century England, where lords and large farmers took over common land, dispossessed the peasants of their common property and created the working class: people who have nothing to sell but their ability to work. For Marx, capitalism isn't a market place full of opportunities, it's generalized theft. The power to control factories and offices is what gives capital control over the labor of workers.

Proudhon versus Marx

Marx developed his understanding of capitalism by debating Pierre Joseph Proudhon, a contemporary anarchist philosopher.[4] For Proudhon the problem was not exploitation but how the market was run. In his ideal system, workers had a right to own their own land and tools but nothing more. This was the source of Proudhon's famous maxim "property is theft." The very existence of large–scale property meant it was stolen: the property–owners had gotten hold of someone else's labor. From there, the large owners could gain a monopoly and undersell smaller competitors.

But merchant greed could be regulated through controlling supply and demand. Proudhon created another maxim to express this fine balance: "suppress property while maintaining possession." Once the large producers were reigned in, small ones would prosper; freed of the desire to grow large, they wouldn't overcharge. Each person would possess enough to trade but not to oppress others. This would lead to a fair marketplace, where prices would represent workers' and merchants' costs. Knowledge and freedom, "the liberty of the contracting parties and the equivalence of the products exchanged" ensured equal exchange. This would "revolutionize law, government, economy, and institutions... (and) drive evil from the face of the earth."

The concept of equal exchange rests on a labor theory of value. This assumes that the work that goes into making commodities can be measured directly, and therefore workers can be paid equal wages. Schumacher criticized Marx for making a "devastating error when he formulated the so–called 'labor theory of value'": by believing wealth only comes from people's activity, Marx succumbed to human–centric arrogance. However, Marx was saying the opposite: capital is anti–human precisely because it only values people for the products they make. He also pointed out a more fundamental problem with the theory: it was inconsistent. Smith, Ricardo and Proudhon couldn't measure labor. If all commodities were measured by the value of their labor, how much was labor itself worth? It couldn't cost itself. The logic was circular; there had to be something else involved.

Marx identified two different types of work: first, concrete labor produces objects with particular uses, such as bread or a computer. This gives an object its use–value: its concrete, sensuous, material qualities. However, there's a near–infinite variety of goods, production times and techniques. A baker's work has to be made equal to a programmer's, otherwise supply and demand breaks down. In other words, for a capitalist market to function, qualitatively different use–values have to be able to exchange.

But how to determine what those use–values are worth? If people get paid for how many hours they put into a job, then the longer they take to finish, the more they earn. Obviously the labor market doesn't work like that. Marx coined the concept Socially Necessary Abstract Labor Time (SNALT): the average amount of time it takes to make a commodity, given the particular social and economic conditions of the workers involved. Capitalists aren't actually buying labor; they're buying labor power i.e. the *time* of the workers themselves. As Marx puts it, "one man during an hour is worth just as much as another man during an hour. Time is everything, man is nothing; he is, at the most, time's carcase (sic). Quality no longer matters. Quantity alone decides everything." Units of workers' time are valuable; the actual units i.e. humans aren't.

Every capitalist tries to lower the time it takes to produce: if a commodity embodies less value but sells at the same market price, more surplus value can go into profits rather than production. This makes SNALT a form of violence inflicted on workers' ability to create. However, humans aren't machines, and the most important part of SNALT is what's *socially* necessary: the ideas, history and culture that shape what it costs for workers to sustain and reproduce themselves. What makes Marx a humanist is his insistence that people, and not machines or technically–defined portions of labor, create value.

The premises of equal exchange are wrong, because Proudhon and the classical economists weren't considering the social basis of the market. The market doesn't exchange concrete use–values, only abstract ones: real values fluctuate above and below market prices. There's no correct "proportional relation" of labor hours in a commodity, there's only a movement of prices based on the battle over SNALT. In fact, the competitive market is essential for prices to reflect SNALT in capitalism and can't be ignored. Artisans who try to trade directly, bypassing market signals, having trouble finding buyers; those who ignore SNALT and produce higher–cost goods will be undersold. "What is left of this 'proportional relation' (of fair price)?" Marx asks. "Nothing but the pious wish of an honest man who would like commodities to be produced in proportions... (to allow) their being sold at an honest price."

An extremely short history of capitalism

A fair wage and price, market access, ethical small businesses... these should sound familiar. The trade union, Fair Trade and localist movements all owe something to Proudhon. But he didn't invent the ideal market economy; the concept extends back to antiquity. Aristotle's ideal economy was based on the exchange of useful goods, and he too condemned usury and money lending. In the Middle Ages Aquinas named a just price for goods and attacked merchant greed. These weren't coincidences; rather, their ideas reflected the pre-capitalist economies both men lived in, where the concentration of wealth came from usury or brute force.

But well before Proudhon or Marx, the conditions for an honest price were fast disappearing as capitalism grew. There's a long, complex debate on what caused capitalism: was it the growth of wage–labor, commodity production or the rise of money? In fact it's all of these things, but more importantly, it's the *domination* of these forms, as they expand and destroy what came beforehand. It's that systemization that turns capital into capital*ism*.

With the advent of widespread European colonization, trade arose for the exclusive pursuit of profit. Economics reflected this: mercantilist economics modeled capitalism as a system for trading commodities, not use–values. Quesnay and the Physiocrats thought the perfect economy was an agricultural one that produced for profit. Local production for use–values was already becoming obsolete in seventeenth century Europe; it disappeared as a major economic force in the nineteenth century, when large–scale industry began to both meet and create demand. Dispossessed from the land, workers had to sell their labor power to survive. Great cities, factories and new firms arose. Capitalists grew large to undersell other capitalists. Equal exchange was swept aside by the oligopolies that dominate today's global market. This was reflected in the ideas of classical political economy. As capitalism came to organize production, Smith and Ricardo made the market into a natural, eternal economy. It's easy to see why: for them, the competitive forces capitalism unleashed inspired the best workers to save their money and become owners. Therefore those at the top deserved to be there.

It's also easy to see why Proudhon, as an anarchist, opposed this development, but Marx took him to task for not under-standing capitalist history and espousing what Marx called feudal socialism. Proudhon was hostile to modern–day working class social movements. He felt that if workers won higher wages they would provoke inflation. This would frighten the ruling class, whose job was to implement his carefully planned equal exchange schemes. It followed that he opposed trade unions and thought the eight–hour workday imposed unfair limits on contract rights. By abolishing monopoly and create truly free trade, Proudhon felt that the working class could overcome capital and the state, but it wasn't allowed to take power for itself. His future society was a series of voluntary contracts based on free commodity exchange, but there was no one left to make and trade those commodities. People couldn't go back to making and trading their own products, because capital controlled the markets and the means of production. It had dispossessed most people from the land, creating the working class and under-mining the basis for small–scale, equal exchange economies.

Marx didn't just describe how capitalism destroyed earlier economies; he predicted how it would grow. Once it became dominant, capital began to concentrate and centralize. Early on, capitalists invested their profits to generate more capital, concen-trating wealth into bigger, individual firms. Later those firms combined in fewer, bigger ones to conquer national and, eventually, international markets. The centralized firms bought machines, raised productivity and generated ever–bigger funds of capital. Small firms continued to exist, of course, but the dominance of centralized capital was firmly established.

Capital remained largely in national boundaries at first, not because of ethical capitalists or capital controls, but because firms lacked safe venues for international investments. To open up those venues, the political maps of Europe and the poor countries of the world, broadly defined as the Global South, were redrawn. The establishment of white settler colonies allowed new direct investments outside Europe and repatriated huge profits. States and the firms they supported took over firms in other countries, or companies merged directly. The number of firms shrank in the face of growing monopolies. Colonial campaigns and two world wars arose as different powers jockeyed for international influence and markets. These pressures only increased after World War II. Capital continued to centralize across borders: new technologies needed such large initial investments that they also required international markets to generate profits. Large–scale production managed to make goods so cheaply that national industries withered and the multinational corporation (MNC) rose to prominence. This fed international capital flows and intra–firm trade within corporations.

Today, MNCs introduce new products at massive volumes to maintain sales and justify capital expenses. This creates further pressure for centralization. Everything's internationalized: production, sales, work and ownership. But this doesn't make states irrelevant; on the contrary, they have a big role to play. Corporations can only grow by ruthlessly cutting costs, and a good way to do that is to shift them onto the public sector: profits remain private, while the state assumes the costs of infrastructure and social welfare. When profit falls, state subsidies to business can offset those potential crises. Localists often see subsidies as policy mistakes by bad politicians, but this suggests business and the state are separate, neutral entities. In fact, they're different arms of capital. When one gets into trouble, the other will step in to maintain growth. As the 2008 bank bailouts demonstrate, no one throws $20 trillion away on a whim: the point is to protect the integrity of the system as a whole and get it growing again.

This growth isn't linear or stable. When a particular sector of the economy becomes profitable, capitalists scramble to enter it. If they don't, they'll be swallowed up by other capitalists who will. This dynamic forces capitalists to expand to undercut their competitors, whether there's a need for their products or not. A crisis occurs again, not because there's no use for all the new goods, but because they can't be sold profitably. Smaller capitalists go under, and large capitalists force down production costs to stay solvent.

This short account just scratches the surface of the last few hundred years of capitalist growth. But it destroys the idea that it's possible to recreate small–scale development in today's advanced capitalist economy. Small business has a role to play, as we'll see, but it's not dominant and never will be, not because politicians are biased against them but because capitalism has to grow or die. Once workers have been dispossessed from the means of production, and a global market in commodities established, value gets determined according to abstract labor or SNALT. That persistent drive to lower costs, and not ethics or the desire for a just price, limits what can be achieved locally.

Contrast this analysis to the localist ethical economy. Capital is a thing: knowledge, infrastructure and equipment, as Schumacher describes it. As localist author Lyle Estill says, "trade is based on 'things', not money," and ultimately on the trust we have for one another. The capital of the natural world is simply a bigger version of what humans make. Ethics replaces social science; once freed of the wrong, profit–hungry impulses, planning and freedom can find their proper balance. The economy achieves a happy equilibrium based on what Schumacher calls a "middle way that reconciles the opposites without degrading them both." Ecological economists Herman Daly and Joshua Farley have a program to limit distribution and growth, but they call for social justice to be imposed on the market, which is supposed to meekly accept and adjust its prices accordingly.

These are examples of economists criticizing their field from the inside. While they see the consequences of capitalism in its irrational growth, they accept its foundations of market rule without question. If capitalism is just a market for things, it can be transformed through organizational change. Marx had little time for those who mistook social for technical relations and tried to avoid the historical evidence of theft and struggle: "the respectable conscience refuses to see this obvious fact... For the bourgeois, individual exchange can exist without any antag-onism of classes. For him, these are two quite unconnected things." Trade, fair or otherwise, is built on exploitation and class conflict.

Capitalism degrades humanity and the natural environment, and the onus is on those who observe the system's contradictions to be clear on both their causes and solutions. Localism has grown out of that degradation, yet no localist has ever answered the questions Marx posed for classical political economists and Proudhon. Marx may have engaged them in bitter intellectual and political warfare, but he would have granted them one concession: they gave an honest account of their political economy. They all thought it was essential to explain how value was created. It was a capitalist innovation to decide that question didn't matter, ignoring value theory in favor of technical questions of supply and demand. Localism also refuses to provide a systematic explanation of value, and in doing so, creates plans for local alternatives that don't challenge the injustices of capitalism.

Chapter Two

Local Visions, Global Realities

Localism has developed into many different streams, which can be roughly grouped into localists who support capitalism and those who want to overcome it. Pro–market localists suggest that market regulation can create ethical local capitalism. Some build small businesses, while others promote non–profits and cooperatives. Locally–owned businesses are supposed to keep money in local communities and, since they're small, treat workers and the environment better. Residents care more about what goes on, participate in local issues and send their kids to local schools. Personal connections can overcome the impersonal, alienating power of the marketplace.

Anti–market localists blame capitalism for separating and isolating us. Instead, people who live close together can create a healthy balance of community, individual and environmental needs. By bartering, creating alternative currencies and local credit, localists can create a cooperative, decentralized economy. Participatory Economics (Parecon) and Libertarian Municipalism (LM) create plans for self–governing communities. The permaculture and appropriate technology movements advocate using smaller–scale, accessible tools in those communities' economies. Taking inspiration from pre–colonial societies, bioregionalism uses the land's ecological limits to plan community self–reliance in every area of economic life, reducing and balancing growth. If these measures were generalized, the homogenizing, alienating forces of capital and the nation–state could eventually disappear. We can start small, with community gardens and cycling, but put together, all these measures can create a postcapitalist future.

Pro–market localism

The pro–market localists say that if the economy is just a collection of use–values, then we can make capitalism better by producing fewer, higher–quality goods. Bill McKibben says setting up local economies "will not mean abandoning Adam Smith or doing away with markets. Markets, obviously, work." The challenge is limiting them. Carlos Petrini, founder of the Slow Food movement, assures readers that "it is not my intention to denounce the capitalist system in itself." Markets are good things and they can be regulated, providing they are operated according to principles of social justice. McKibben calls localism "neither 'liberal' or conservative'"; rather, the choice is between increasing production and building community values. Redistribution, sharing the wealth, won't stop the problem of unrestricted growth. The answer is to make the economy less efficient, something both conservatives and environmentalists can agree on because it's not "ideological."

This confusion peaks with markets solving the problems their existence poses. Daly and Farley want to make everything into marketable commodities. Then, by limiting production and distribution, local economies will make goods scarce, more valuable and less liable to be wasted. McKibben calls for more capitalists, demanding governments legalize squatter land rights and the black market to give business owners and squatters more capital. By these definitions, a capitalist is simply an entre-preneur held back by public land rights and red tape. Michael Shuman, a small–business booster, suggests informed consumers demonstrate a preference for small business, which is "woven into the fabric of the community" and less likely to leave. From these assertions, localists make sweeping assumptions about the power of local communities to set laws and regulations that protect their quality of life. Market power either doesn't exist or will mobilize what McKibben calls "good old fashioned greed," providing the high prices necessary to switch to green technology and promote community values. The market will work when it suits the local economy, and be abandoned when it does not, changing selfish politics and values to community–oriented ones. Freed from both bureaucratic barriers and global market prices, capitalists will develop a sense of social responsibility. By remaining in the community, they will find what McKibben calls "a sweet spot" that balances individualism and production. The social relations of capitalism either can't change, don't have to, or don't exist at all: the trajectory of economic growth can be reversed without changing who owns what.

Idealizing the local

Pro–market localists claim the small scale of local business makes it more ethical. Big business separates owners from those who work and consume; bring them together, the localists say, and business will be more personal. David Morris claims that "small is the scale of efficient, dynamic, democratic and environmentally benign societies." As with Proudhon, the key concept is fairness: for Schumacher, exploitation only happens if a business owner takes too much for herself, getting higher interest rates than normal on her capital. Anything extra should be shared with all other co–workers. In these circumstances, labor exploitation no longer matters: "even autocratic control is no serious problem in a small–scale enterprise which, led by a working proprietor, has almost a family character." As long as the business is small, "private ownership is natural, fruitful, and just." Capitalism is fair as long as it's done correctly.

Charles Fourier was a nineteenth century reformer who appealed to the wealthy to fund his ideal communities. Like him, the localists look for good capitalists who refuse to become too rich. Although most capitalists corrupt themselves through greed and envy, Schumacher finds one who "refused to become inordinately rich and thus made it possible to build a real *community*."

McKibben praises a Chinese rabbit–farmer who, inspired by an aid group that gave him start–up capital (i.e. rabbits) "then became a kind of philanthropist, spending most of his wealth and time training others." Enlightened small businesspeople can divest their holdings and give ownership to their employees. Petrini advocates "friendship and the joining of forces over economic competition, the public over the private, the gift over trade." For Kingsolver, in the face of corporate concentration in agriculture, the answer "for both growers and the consumers who care, is a commitment to more local food economies." Profit can be made optional by caring about the proper, local size.

This points to a key confusion at the heart of localism: it conflates the size of ownership with the size of production. The two are very different: while larger *production* needs concentrations of machinery and labor power, larger *ownership* doesn't. Some localists look to technology to create local production, and it's true that high–tech can create smaller factories that internalize more parts of the production process, bringing it under local control. Computerization has shrunk tasks that previously required a vast commodity chain. Small–batch production can be mechanized. The notion of ever–bigger factories with more and more workers is false, but centralized ownership is big and getting bigger. Confusing facilities with ownership allows localists to echo Adam Smith's promotion of small, equal capitals. Opposed to a capitalism controlled by monopolies, Smith believed that markets could be self–regulating and competitive if producers and consumers were kept small. Smith had the benefit of describing his own historical period: during the eighteenth century, small companies battled it out to control local markets. Not today: small business is less and less important to directing economic activity.

Going by the numbers alone, small business plays a central role in American capitalism. In 2007, almost 22 million Americans were self–employed, while 5.4 million businesses employed 20 workers or less, generating 49% of all new jobs. This compared to just over 18,000 firms of 500 or more employers, meaning small firms collectively made up 99.7% of employers, not including unpaid volunteer and household work or the informal market. But just citing these figures misses the economic weight of those 18,000 firms. By 1870, corporations had grown into monopoly capitalist enterprises that controlled entire markets and were powerful enough to set prices all other businesses had to meet. Today monopoly has grown into oligopoly, where corporations not only control national markets but global supply chains. As early as 1973, monopoly corporations employed a third of all American workers. Now they employ over half: capitalist economies are moving towards monopoly, not away from it.

This doesn't mean small business will disappear. It can create new industries and new kinds of production in existing ones. When crises wipe out existing capital, big capital is happy to let smaller firms rebuild industries. But in the long run, small capital loses: since capitalists compete to undersell each other, the scale of ownership constantly increases. The minimum amount of capital necessary for new business increases, while the time available for smaller capital to invest decreases. Small capitalists get priced out of the market. Moreover, since profits tend to fall over time, there is a strong tendency towards small capitals with lower operating reserves being driven bankrupt, although some manage to survive.

There are two other technical problems with small production facilities. First, commodities may cost more than products made in bigger facilities. If they rely on high–cost, niche markets to sell their products, firms shrink their customer base to wealthy consumers and can limit their survivability. Second, small production doesn't necessarily solve environmental problems. Miniaturization still requires vast amounts of resources, such as the carbon and water required for precise, water– and laser–cut components. Smaller firms have to use more energy and resources to create their own production chains. They also may not be able to afford environmental protection measures. In the United Kingdom, a report found that of small businesses voluntarily reporting environmental protection measures, only 28% of firms with less than 10 employees created any at all. This compared with 77% of businesses with 50 to 250 employees that implemented measures. Only 70% of chemicals businesses had regulations in place, the highest compliance of any sector. Just under half of electronics firms had green measures; only 31% of metals and 30% of textile industries participated. Most small businesses did not have a comprehensive, organization–wide Environmental Management System or plans to introduce one. The report concluded: "whether or not a business had an environmental policy depended critically on size. Smaller businesses were least likely to… safeguard the environment."

The ethics of small businesses start looking uncertain, because they're under constant pressure from monopolies. The smaller they are, the more their products cost, because production and distribution also costs more. Contrary to reputation, this makes them less likely to be environmentally friendly. What about the impact of small business on the community and workers?

Does local money stay in local spaces?

One of the most common localist claims is that locally–owned businesses create a virtuous circle, keeping money in the community. This claim was investigated empirically by Civic Economics, a consulting firm hired by businesses in Andersonville, a Chicago neighborhood, to compare the impact of local commerce versus chain stores. The survey found that "ten local firms generate a combined $6.7 million in annual economic impact compared to $8.8 million for the ten chains." However, the disaggregated data shows a net benefit to the local economy. For every $100 consumers spend at chain stores, $43 stays in the local community, while spending at locally–owned stores retains $68. The "local economic impact" of chain stores equals $105 per square foot, versus $179 for locally–owned stores. While chain stores pull in more revenue, they have more square footage too, so their comparative economic advantage is wiped out: small stores pack more value into a smaller space. This is called a Local Premium: how much more revenue remains local in locally–owned firms versus foreign ones. Local service providers keep 90% more money locally than chains, retailers 63% and restaurants 27%.

However, this isn't as straightforward as it seems. First, for local money to stay in the community, all production must be local. As we've seen, local merchants aren't truly local if the goods they're selling are imported. Suggesting, as Shuman does, that local businesses mainly provide services, not goods, doesn't solve this problem. Even the most service–based small businesses still need an infrastructure of foreign–made products to support them: massage therapists need tables, web designers need computers, and so on. Money may circulate locally for a single stage, from consumer to merchant, but spreads very quickly afterwards.

Second, these figures conceal technical problems. The study claims that since eight out of 10 local firms are owned by Chicagoans, the money stays in the city: locally–owned businesses purchase local goods "at more than twice the rate of chains." But Chicago is a big place: what if the money leaves Andersonville and goes to a business owner living in the tony Gold Coast neighborhood? It may cost more to transport goods into a locality than to make and sell those goods locally, although that depends on transportation technologies that capital is continually transforming. But spending more locally can backfire. If goods cost more at the mom–and–pop shop than at Wal–Mart, then total, net consumption goes down: higher prices lower the level of goods and services consumed overall, leaving less money to be spent locally. Likewise, the money saved at Wal–Mart could be spent locally. As well, if local spending in rich localities stays there, then it just aggravates inequality with poor neighborhoods. There's no clear equation of local shopping with a fairer economy.

Third, the argument relies on neoclassical assumptions about where wealth comes from. The authors explain that "local economic impacts for businesses that serve a local market are primarily made up of four components: labor, profit, procurement, and charity." Labor becomes a wage cost while profits simply "remain in the city." According to neoclassical economics, these are all factors and outcomes of production, and the study assumes all members of a local community derive equal impacts from paying wages, purchasing supplies and earning profits: in other words, that they are all entrepreneurs. Yet according to Marx, labor is the sole source of profit, procurement and corporate charity, from which workers earn nothing.

The importance of labor is suggested by the study's own figures: the 70 percent Local Premium of local businesses "are largely accounted for by one factor: labor costs." However, this doesn't mean that small, local firms pay their workers more. Shuman hints at their work conditions where many home–based businesses comprise second and third jobs, suggesting workers become entrepreneurs primarily due to stagnant wages. American companies with more than 500 employees pay a third higher wages than smaller ones. Small businesses are signifi- cantly less likely to provide healthcare coverage, a major cost for employees. In Canada, companies with more than 500 workers pay higher weekly wages than medium and small firms with fewer than 500 and 100 workers respectively. As of 2003 the wage–gap between large and small employers had shrunk by a third, caused by overseas production and the growth of low–wage employers. In other words, the wages big business pays are shrinking to the meager, existing level of small ones, which is hardly an argument for the latter. Small production facilities help this along: in fact, capital has introduced smaller, high–tech workplaces to break up concentrations of workers and reduce their bargaining power.

Shuman tries to equate small business's personal management style with a respect for labor rights. Although he acknowledges small businesses are harder to unionize, he hopes for "socially responsible entrepreneurs... who believe that high wages and decent benefits are not just good motivators but also moral imperatives." Thus "labor should embrace small business, unionize it where it can, and encourage worker ownership, participation, and entrepreneurship where it cannot." McRobie echoes this sentiment by speaking approvingly of the Canadian Federation of Independent Business, as "a powerful advocate of small–scale technology and decentralization," despite the CFIB's anti–labor demand for lower public sector wages. The power of moral imperative pales next to the force of SNALT.

So where does the wage premium come from? The Andersonville study finds that locally owned stores pay 28% of their revenue on wages, versus 23% for chains. But this finding appears to collapse owner–operators and employers of small firms together. As the study states, local businesses "are heavily dependent on the labors of the owner... resulting in the most substantial Local Premium." These results appear elsewhere. In Austin, Texas, local businesses retained 45 cents of every dollar in the city, while the Borders book chain retained 13 cents. The gap was "mostly in the form of wages. Most of the difference came from profits... but the local businesses also spent a higher percentage of revenue on wages, partly because of higher pay rates, and partly because of less efficient staffing." A Local Premium becomes a code for small businesspeople working longer hours and incurring higher wage costs, forced to duplicate administrative tasks that large firms can centralize.

Robin Hahnel argues that idealizing small business is simply a form of nostalgia for earlier forms of capitalism, which weren't necessarily any better. Small, family–owned businesses also pay poor wages, price–gouge customers and destroy the environment. Interestingly, as of 2010 US small business owners were 83 percent white, married, older men. That figure shrank only four percent from 2000. This means that the small business culture localists defend is also fairly exclusive. These trends suggest, at the very least, that small firms aren't inherently better for workers than large ones.

As Marx wrote, labor creates value and capital appropriates it. To lower costs, capitalists have to shrink the value that each commodity contains. They do this by introducing machines and efficiency savings, tasks that local businesses don't have the capital to accomplish. The Local Premium comes from small businesses owners substituting their own bodies and time for capital. This may be viable, but it's a huge amount of effort for not very much reward. It's not an escape from the global law of value or a vision for a friendlier, more humane community.

Consumers in capitalism

To buttress these plans, localists depend on ethical consumers. Small business goods might cost more, but people who care can pay more. This gives a lot of power to consumers; yet it's not clear that consumers are all that powerful to begin with.

According to neoclassical economics, a consumer is an informed individual, making rational decisions in the market to maximize her self–interest. There's no surplus, growth is an accident of production and capital comes from investors beating the odds for a while. Workers and owners are just temporary categories; we're really just individuals who come to market to meet our infinite needs, and some of us are lucky enough have extra cash on hand to sell goods to others. The market can either

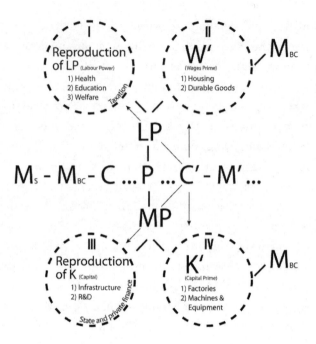

Figure 1: Circuits of Consumption

self–regulate or get by with a little help from the government. By demonstrating a preference for particular goods, consumers can change the way those goods are produced and distributed.

In reality this doesn't describe most people, who consume according to standard patterns socialized through culture and family. However, it does describe capitalists, who buy and sell on the market to increase their monopoly over labor power. To look at this analysis a little closer, it helps to draw on Marx's algebra.[5] Before capitalism, there was no global market. People created commodities (C), which they exchanged for money (M), which was used to buy other commodities: C – M – C. This describes a steady–state economy with no growth. It's also obsolete. Today, capital is in constant motion. As Marx writes in *The Communist Manifesto*, "Constant revolutionizing of production, uninter-rupted disturbance of all social conditions, everlasting uncertainty and agitation distinguish the bourgeois epoch from all earlier ones." Consumers don't drive this process. This doesn't mean consumption is irrelevant: in a strictly technical sense, our needs create all economic activity. But production determines what shape consumption takes and creates new needs. Figure One is a snapshot of that process.

In the middle row, money is separated out into Speculative capital (M_s) and bank capital (M_{bc}), which provide the initial investment to create commodities (C) in the production process (P). Through the purchase of the Means of Production (MP) and the exploitation of Labor Power (LP), surplus value is created, appropriated and made into more commodities (C') and money (M'). Commodities are sold in different spheres, M' gets fed back into production and the loop continues. It rarely works as it's supposed to: speculation, raw materials shortages and strikes can interrupt profit–making. But let's give the capitalists their due and pretend there are perfect–world conditions, where all investment in production gets realized, earning a profitable return through consumption. Production gets consumed in two forms: the MP, where capital reproduces itself, and LP, in which workers reproduce themselves. If this seems like an unfeeling way to talk about work, remember that from the point of view of capital, workers are just labor power and nothing more.

Capital in MP can go into Circuit III, where the state and private firms invest in infrastructure and research and development (R&D). In Circuit IV, private capital takes care of itself, using surplus value to expand and replace factories and equipment. But for our purposes, LP is most important. In Circuit I, the state provides social services to help workers take care of themselves. Today this is mostly paid for by taxes on workers. We finally get to consumption In Circuit II. It contains Wages Prime (W'), the net wages of the working class, who spend most of their income on housing and durable goods. Consumer spending is a form of distribution, part of the circuit of exchange. It represents the reproduction of workers' own labor power, not control over the entire process.

The capitalist comes onto the market as a consumer of labor power. Neoclassical economics focuses on consumers, and this reflects reality... for the capitalist. But it also means that any economic theory beginning with consumers, consumption or exchange adopts the capitalist's own point of view. Figure One shows why this won't work, for two reasons.

First, wages don't create all demand: they're just one way for capitalists to realize the capital invested in commodities, C'. There are three other circuits that supply public and private goods at all stages of the creation and reproduction of LP and MP. Most people encounter the market when they shop, so it seems natural to believe that capitalism exists to satisfy our consumer needs. But while the market in consumer goods is constantly on display, exploitation is hidden. Workers matter as *workers*, the source of surplus value: they're only able to receive and spend a wage if their employer makes a profit first. Moreover, capitalist production creates capital goods that only business buys: the machinery and building materials that go into factories, offices and other sites of exploitation. Capital has to consume materials at all stages of the production process. Machines increase production, making more machines necessary and increasing the importance of industries producing the means of production. There are huge areas of the economy off–limits to workers' spending power.

The state and capital also consume much of the social product on their own. The capitalist strives to make commodities easier to sell by introducing machines into the production process, removing the need for labor, putting downward pressure on wages and lowering prices. However, this sets limits on how much consumers can purchase, while at the same time creating larger volumes that need to be sold. The existence of more goods, with fewer people to buy them, creates a potential crisis and forces capital to consume ever–larger portions of the social product itself. The more developed a capitalist society becomes, the more consumption shifts progressively away from individual consumers and towards firms.

Second, money capital funds every circuit: it not only provides start–up capital but helps workers' wages circulate by providing personal credit, increasing capital through banks and corporate self–financing. M_s and M_{bc} are just two examples: new forms of credit continue to spawn, both because industries self–finance and because speculators can suck up surplus value that can't be reinvested profitably. To influence this process, consumers would have to find some way of controlling investment decisions at all stages of capital circulation, including private investment and state purchase of goods. Otherwise, capitalists would pull investment dollars from the more expensive, less technically developed, ethical local industries.

The idea that workers could control the circuit of capital repeats Ricardo's error by assuming workers receive the full value of their labor, rather than the price of their labor power in production. However, Figure One shows how the surplus value that workers hand over to the boss is the actual source of capital and commodities. Even if localist missionaries convinced all workers that local consumption could change the world, workers could, at best, change the conditions of production for their own housing and durable goods, a small portion of the capital circuit.

Ethical consumption

Despite these limits, wages are the focus for all pro–market localist schemes. If consumers buy locally–sourced goods from ethical sellers, they'll shrink the economy to a more rational, sustainable level. It's a truism that we in the West consume too much. People buy what they don't need or too much of what they do. Businesses relying on individual consumers spend vast amounts to convince them that their lives are incomplete without the latest gadget. Consumers who reject mass consumption often get drawn into their own form of elitism, paying huge sums for the coffee and gadgets that define their counter–cultural cachet.

Localists frame this by aggregating individual consumption choices: as Kingsolver says of the US, "in a country where 5 percent of the world's population glugs down a quarter of all the fuel... we've apparently made big choices about consumption." It's assumed that we've all chosen, on our own, to consume too much fuel, and this individualism marks localist thinking. Petrini says, "the time has come for everybody – producers, traders, institutions, associations, and individual citizens – to ask themselves whether their lifestyle is sustainable." These individual choices, put together, will change the system. McKibben doesn't "foresee a coordinated change in our economies, but a gradual one... pulled by personal desire" and environmental needs. Making numerous small choices will add up to changing big ones. Consumers can change not only their spending habits but entire industries. Shuman names 10 different areas shoppers could buy locally, imagining a consumer–led panacea of local business, finance and technology to bring the community together "to envision a better economic future for all of its members." Petrini's Slow Food movement creates a model economy where producers teach consumers about production and distribution, consumers create new food communities, and together they create a market in the "exchange of abilities," trading their work in a growing, alternative system of community distribution. Consumers can recreate a smaller, parallel, nicer capitalism.

But capitalism does a lot more than offer different products for us to buy. The market coordinates production for an entire society, which makes it very hard to recreate in miniature. For example, localists acknowledge that the quality of local food isn't consistent. It's hard to get and often costs more, both because of economies of scale and because its production and distribution aren't subsidized. Consumers are supposed to compensate for this by paying more. With the Hundred Mile Diet, Smith and MacKinnon decided to consume only food that came from the local watershed. Yet they had to visit numerous grocery stores, sourcing every ingredient and paying $128.87 for a single local meal. No food out of season was allowed, eliminating staples like rice and wheat grain. They ate potatoes for most meals.

Addressing these problems, Kingsolver suggests we produce fruit, vegetables and livestock locally as well, "to exercise some control over which economy we would support." But when Smith and MacKinnon switched to growing their own food, it added a burden of work. If they bought rather than grew food, it required calculations to figure out its degree of localness. In another example, after a week spent tracing the origin of his Thanksgiving dinner, Estill still couldn't figure out food miles for all 34 ingredients.

The problem is that a capitalist economy is simply too complex for individuals to understand, let alone change at a micro level. For example, in a bid to reduce greenhouse gases, localists trace a major source of the carbon footprint through transportation, and a 2001 American study states that shipping food nationally uses 17 times more fuel than regional shipping. More recent research suggests food travels 2500 miles on average before purchase. Therefore localists advocate locally-grown produce to reduce food miles. However, certain foodstuffs are more carbon-intensive when grown in industrialized countries, because their colder climate means more carbon is used for storage. Spanish tomato farmers produce less carbon dioxide than British farmers, while Kenyan rose producers emit less carbon dioxide than the Dutch. Production creates 83 percent of food-related carbon emissions, transportation only 11 percent. In fact, transportation can be so efficient that it uses less carbon than local goods: for example, large-scale container and rail shipping means importing frozen fish uses less carbon than breeding fresh local fish. The distance between farm and market isn't an accurate gauge of environmental costs. And since those costs are external to the consumer anyways, consumers won't pay extra for them.

How can consumers study the life cycle of each item in their shopping cart, particularly when it's often hidden? The answer, according to Petrini, is that "one must not give in; one must reconsider and redefine the role of the consumer." Yet even economists can't create models that account for the supply and demand of goods and services in an advanced capitalist economy. For Daly and Farley, trying to map interrelated production and distribution networks results in a "thousand simultaneous equations with a thousand unknowns (that) is hard to come into mental contact with… it is also crippling… to face the implication that in order to predict anything, you have first to know every-thing." This is, of course, impossible; but buried in what seems like a technical limitation, the economists are grappling with the irrationality of an economy based on demand and supply to signal what's needed. A commodity's life cycle is incredibly complex and hidden, and getting more so every day; even if its impact is clear, there may not other alternatives available. But rather than democratically plan the economy, allowing social need and not profit to dictate what gets made and how, consumers are supposed to refuse to "give in" and cope individ-ually with market anarchy.

If ethical consumption relies on consumer preferences, then consumers can equally choose not to participate. In a system where consumers are workers with nothing to sell except their labor power, it's rational to buy goods as cheaply as possible. And this is what happens when capitalism goes into crisis. From 1999 to 2009, UK spending on ethical products rose from £13,500,000,000 to £43,200,000,000. Clearly, consumers with disposable income can consume ethically. However, they are still bounded by the market. The effect of the 2008 recession was ambiguous: on the one hand Fair Trade spending continued its ten year growth from £22 million to £749 million annual sales. The overall ethical goods market increased 18 percent despite the recession. However, organic food sales suffered: after peaking at 2 percent of total sales, overall sales volume fell in 2008, with a 19 percent drop in the first three months of 2009. Eight farmers dropped organic certification every week. It was not, as farmers and environmentalists hoped, a blip, as most shoppers planned to reduce their organic, ethical and Fair Trade consumption even after the recession ended. Discount supermarkets were the main beneficiaries of shoppers' loyalties.

Ethical consumption remains popular: after all, it's a way to feel you're changing the world by spending a little extra. But the question is whether it's actually changing the production and distribution circuits of capital. UK ethical consumption represents less than 1 percent of total household spending. At what point will the number of ethical consumers peak, when those with no disposable income can't participate? And, since it can't change the global drive to reduce costs below the average global price, what distinguishes ethical consumption from charity, a way to salve the consciences of the well-to-do, leaving the structures creating inequality intact and growing?

The assumption behind consumer activism is that we're limited to shopping to express our discontent. This is effectively saying the neoclassical economists are right: the economy runs on consumer preferences, not exploitation. This shifts blame onto individual consumers for the failings of the system: if there's alienation and environmental misery, it's your fault for buying the wrong things. Yet consumers are also workers who must sell their labor power or lose their homes and livelihoods. They buy what makes their wages stretch further. From the capitalist's point of view, providing cheaper goods allows them to pay workers less, as Marx wrote: "In a society founded on *poverty* the poorest products have the fatal prerogative of being used by the greatest number." They're not more useful, in terms of providing nutrition or health. But then, capitalism provides profits first and useful things second.

In fact, the vast majority of people in the world need to consume *more*. You read that correctly. Given the excess of cars and appliances filling our roads and homes, it may seem obvious that growth is a bad thing. But for the vast majority of people, capitalism isn't meeting their needs. In the Global North, only those lucky enough to have a job can pay for essential needs like transportation, education and healthcare. In the Global South, billions of people live on less than $2 a day. In this context, calling for people to consume less misses the point. Real ethical consumption is *collective*. Capitalism makes it impossible for most people to meet their needs on their own, but as a society, we could provide houses, hospitals and schools for all. The only reason shoddy merchandise gets made is because capital creates a market for the people it underpays. Redistribute wealth and consumption could skyrocket, as everything from public transportation to musical instruments got used communally, while poor quality, useless items wouldn't find any demand. Obviously this implies a vast change in the structure of ownership and consumption, but it's a far more positive vision than localism's individualism.

Anti–market localism and the problem of autonomy

These limitations point to the need to overcome the market, in order to create socially useful production. Schumacher was not opposed to socialism, and radical, anarchist localisms are explicitly anti–capitalist. Anti–market localisms have developed a more complex relationship between the political and economic; rather than trying to play by market rules, they focus on experiments in decentralization and community–controlled democracy. However, while these localisms criticize the effects of capitalist development, their alternatives don't provide many answers.

Anti-market localism calls on communities to de-link from international economies so they can respond better to local needs. It's true that some products are best made locally: for instance, in temperate climates, some food can be grown closer to where it's eaten. Large-scale production and transport often relies on environmentally damaging infrastructure, with the 2010 oil spill disaster in the Gulf of Mexico and the 2011 nuclear disaster in Fukushima being only the latest examples.

But by turning de-linking into a principle, localism assumes everything that society makes can be reproduced locally. Marx called this the Robinson Crusoe theory of history: even the things that Crusoe used to survive, stuck on his island far from anyone, were the product of a widespread social division of labor. In fact, from the Neolithic era onwards, individual communities have never been self-sufficient economically, and farmers and artisans have relied on outside resources for tools and raw materials. A good way to understand this is by viewing production as a series of chains, stringing together labor and productive processes to manufacture, transport and market commodities. Although mineral deposit and agriculture-based economies are heavily place-dependent, extracting, creating and transporting market commodities across vast spaces have shaped economies for thousands of years. Production has *never* been entirely local; trying to force it to become so creates serious problems.

The first issue is wasteful duplication. Shuman points out that a windmill producing power for a locality would still need a steel industry to build it and supply parts. Otherwise the locality would have to build other products for export, in order to generate currency to buy materials. As he says, this "process of substitution never ends." There would be no reason for communities to duplicate products when other places could make them more efficiently. If localities did specialize, then capital would move to where goods could be produced the cheapest and production would no longer be local.

The second issue is coordination: if local jurisdictions had to recreate every industry, it would be impossible to meet the needs of a technologically advanced society. Without social planning and a mechanism to distribute production between communities, exclusively local production would be incredibly inefficient and worsen inequality. Bioregionalism, which designates a geographic boundary around a self–sufficient region, is a good example of these problems, because it fails to account for the complexities of human development. Decisions would still have to be made about where people live, how land gets redistributed, who gets to use it and how to reconcile the interests of capitalist property with people. It's not clear how the resulting conflicts would be resolved differently than any other recent war over resources.

Shuman argues for Import Substitution Industrialization (ISI): localities should create new facilities to produce goods for trade with other local communities, saving money that previously would have been spent on imports. Global price volatility could be avoided by producing for neighbors, not for international export. Yet the demands of a global market have scuttled previous attempts at ISI. In the post World War II era, countries in the Global South attempted to develop their own industrial base, creating finished manufacturing goods for home use rather than importing them using expensive foreign currency. This large–scale social engineering depended on wealth and property redistribution to build new national industries, a process often resisted by local elites with vested interests in existing industries. Even successful ISI nations still faced a huge technological gap between their own level of development and that of the capital–rich states, which they depended upon for expertise and supplies. When states tried to tax transnationals and put the proceeds towards national development, companies closed down and moved or started transfer pricing, shifting profit–reporting to lower–taxed subsidiaries elsewhere. The goods ISI industries did produce were still subject to the vagaries of global commodity prices and often couldn't compete with products from more developed states. The industries and home markets had to be protected through tariffs and subsidies, creating massive debts. When the World Bank and International Monetary Fund stepped in to provide aid to indebted nations, they demanded the end of those protective financial measures.

This was not just a question of problems inherent in the economies of the Global South. ISI encounters even more problems in advanced capitalist economies that, unlike poorer states, can't import existing production and distribution models and must establish new ones to remain competitive. Governments can nationalize existing industries or set up new ones, but capital is just as interested in retaining control in rich nations as in poor ones. Setting up national industries, to say nothing of local ones would require restricting private property rights. ISI was a partial, temporary de–linking from the global market to establish a more competitive national economy. These plans failed even with vast amounts of capital and power behind them. Localism aims to recreate this autarky on an even flimsier basis, as a moral rather than nationalist project. Local production is not about choosing the proper size of production and social organization, but a social question of capital's power to dictate what gets made and how.

What's wrong with high–tech?

As with ownership and factory size, localism also conflates the size of industry with the technology it uses. There's no automatic correlation: as shown, large–scale owners can create high–tech production that's also small. However, there is still a relationship: particular industries have adopted machines to create economies of scale and become more efficient. For example, industrial farming generates seven times as much output with a third of the labor force compared to farming 100 years ago. Localists recognize that the growth of technology, as part of unrestrained economic growth, can create an unsustainable social and ecological impact, for which they blame industrial society as a whole.

The argument begins, quite rightly, with a sense that capitalism degrades everyday life. Schumacher blames "crudest materialism, for which money costs and money incomes are the ultimate criteria and determinants of human action," for reducing nature to *"a quarry for exploitation."* This closely reflects Marx's own position: if a product from nature has no profitable use, it has no value for capital and becomes what mainstream economics calls an externality. Marx didn't mean nature has no value unless we work on it. Rather, under capitalism, property owners appropriate natural wealth for themselves. The need to generate a profit takes priority over the land and the people who use it.

Schumacher recognizes that, for the sake of profit, industry centralizes and specializes production to save labor, degrading workers' quality of life in the process. Yet because he's trapped in a use–value analysis, for him capitalist degradation stems from the wrong kind of uses: the machine technologies that create industrialism. He goes to great lengths to describe the difference between tools, which he sees as extensions of a worker's hands, and a machine, which is a "mechanical slave." Using expensive and complex machines eliminates poor people's jobs. Schumacher calls instead for the creation of large numbers of small workplaces using cheap, simple technologies and local materials for local consumption.

Marx was acutely conscious of how awful large–scale industry can be, devoting over 100 pages of *Capital Volume One* to describing how machine technology brutalizes workers. However, this wasn't a problem of size or design but purpose: machines exist to replace human workers. Machines create commodities more quickly than people, shortening how long it takes a worker to generate enough value for her wages, and to "lengthen the other part, the part (the worker) gives to the capitalist for nothing." The social purpose of technology is to drive down the value embodied in commodities, making each one cheaper and easier to sell. It is this dynamic, and not the machines themselves, that displaces the poor from their workplaces.

Since that displacement is the purpose of large–scale industry, this also means that it's very hard for the poor to use appropriate technology to work themselves out of poverty. Expensive, large–scale technology is more efficient for capital. There's no clearer sign of this than the vast amounts spent on R&D each year. Production depends on the ability of large units of capital to underwrite risk and adopt new technologies. The division of labor has developed to the point that much of this research involves international collaboration by states, individual researchers and firms locating across borders. Global R&D amounted to over $1.1 trillion USD in 2009, and that number rose in 2010. With the exception of major industrial powers like the US, Japan and China, individual nations' spending is dwarfed by the total. In advanced capitalism, solving the technical problems of production requires vast resources. This makes it unlikely that capital will fund small–scale appropriate technologies that aim to help people, not corporations.

Marx didn't fetishize industrialism. He was the first to explain how capitalism formed by stealing common land from people and he felt that socialism, in redressing this injustice, had to accept the land's natural limits. But 150 years ago, large–scale industry already existed, as an attempt to solve the problems capitalism created. Marx's question was how to organize it. For example, he saw that large–scale industry could also create large–scale recycling. This suggests how contradictory economies of scale are: they make cheaper goods, but their expansion raises the costs of raw materials and technology. With each new technological fix, large–scale production leads to larger–scale production, in order to solve the technical and logistical problems the process creates.

However, just because large–scale production creates environmental and social problems, it doesn't mean the opposite is true: there's no automatic link between appropriate and small technologies. What Murray Bookchin calls "antitechnologism" masks capital accumulation as the cause of irrational growth and exploitation. For example, Schumacher decries slavery as a moral evil. But it was far more than that: slaves were a cheap alternative for the machinery needed to harvest cotton, which was picked, processed and shipped from the colonies by hand. The high–tech industries that localists decry played no part in the slave trade, one of the cruelest acts of human history. As CLR James wrote on San Domingo, the colony that would become Haiti, "Prosperity is not a moral question and the justification of San Domingo was its prosperity." The profit motive, not machinery, created slavery on its own.

Sometimes large–scale, high–tech industries are appropriate too. McRobie claims that a focus on people, and not commodities, would lead to technologies to help poor women. Yet labor–saving devices like laundry machines have the potential to free women from some of that work. Consumer goods, let alone mass public transit systems and high–speed internet, are impossible without a highly–developed capacity to source materials, process them into finished products and distribute them across large distances. For example, making solar panels involves advanced machinery and massive financing that would be impossible to muster locally. The Chinese government provides direct per–watt subsidies for all solar panel producers, as well as absorbing 70 percent of plant–building costs. The question of what kind of growth depends on who wants it. Can it be targeted to help the poor, or will it further concentrate power in the hands of the wealthy?

There are good examples of technology that poor people can use with no other resources than animals and their own physical strength. However, this would be foolish in places with an advanced division of labor. In its current form, high–tech creates vast amounts of waste and pollution, damaging workers and the environment. But green production, such as renewable materials and fuels, could spread the benefits of benign technologies beyond the rich. This suggests democratic social planning: workers in poor countries should be able to decide what kind of development they want. Moreover, socially useful high–tech development is an ethical imperative, since poor countries have borne most of the costs of high–tech as sites of production and disposal. It will cost a lot to make poor societies environmentally sustainable: for example, building high–density development to create viable mass public transit, waste recycling and green fuel distribution. Even localism's direct democracy needs high–tech to reduce people's workload and allow them time to participate. The vast resources harnessed by capitalism need to be studied carefully to see whether they can be put to rational ends, not automatically accepted or rejected.

Anti–market localists extend their criticism of size beyond technology to work and finance. They argue that work can be freeing if it's exchanged directly, and that new, local enterprises can be created using community credit schemes such as alternative local currencies.

Work as freedom

The Marxist vision of freedom is based on workers running society themselves, choosing what gets made and how. This requires ending capitalism, which can only exist as long as capitalists, and not workers, control the labor process and its products. Localists try to implement this vision without changing who owns the means of production, creating small projects of liberated work and freeing participants from what

Schumacher calls the "attachment to wealth." It's true that, as he says, "work, properly conducted in conditions of human dignity and freedom, blesses those who do it." Unemployment isn't just a loss of income but a loss of the "nourishing and enlivening factor of disciplined work." But since when has capitalist work been dignified or nourishing? And who gets to choose not to participate? The confusion comes from mixing up wage–labor and productive activity in general. Marx agrees that labor can be liberating: his earliest work defined being human as the capacity to create. But there's nothing freeing about capitalist labor, because it's forced: workers can't survive by doing anything else.

Only those with enough social power get to choose either not to work if they don't want to, or to work for free in messy but rewarding jobs. Estill lauds "sustainable agriculture," where despite its "excruciatingly labor intensive" nature, "farm interns (are) enjoying a high quality of life despite their low standard of living." The point is not whether this work is enjoyable, which depends on whether you enjoy strenuous farm labor or not, but whether it's available. It's probably true that, as Carrlson says, "un–waged work fulfills and confirms a multidimensional sensibility, providing a whole range of feelings and experiences beyond the narrow instrumentalism of work for money." Without this coercion, Estill adds, "(a)nything's possible, we can manifest any reality we desire." Unfortunately, those without capital, the vast majority of us, have to get by with a unidimensional experience: selling our labor power to survive. We all need to feed, clothe, house and entertain ourselves; without a wage, that becomes very difficult.

LETS, alternative currency and credit schemes

Rather than participating in a global system that gives more power to big corporations, anti–market localism says we can trade what we make directly between each other. This appears in three different reform schemes: Local Exchange Trading Systems

(LETS) systems, which match goods and service providers; local currencies, which create a different store of value that circulates in local spaces; and new forms of credit to support ethical small business.[6]

These harken back to Proudhon's pre–capitalist vision of carpenters, potters and small farmers, sharing what they made before the banks and big capital got involved. For example, when Estill models a small, local economy, he describes artisans in his town painting, growing and teaching yoga for each other, all of whom are on a first–name basis: "at the heart of a vibrant economy is a meaningful living for one." This is the LETS principle: instead of trading goods or services, participants trade IOUs with a promise to provide those goods and services.

LETS work as long as there are enough participants who need the services offered. But the problem with direct barter is that, in most cases, no one is offering what you need when you need it. The smaller the number of participants, the more likely that gap will appear. Market values still dictate LETS values: when the scrip becomes exchangeable with regular money, those who have more currency to begin with do better. Middle–class people provide the high–value, scarce skills that got them their regular jobs, while poor people have to do more labor–intensive tasks. For example, Jeffrey Ingham cites a case where a scrip representing labor–hours was equivalent to $10 US: "lawyers charge five Hours per hour, and babysitters half an Hour per hour." Meeker–Lowry asks those who "want to move away from the conventional value system... should one person's labor be worth three or four times what someone else earns?" Since LETS doesn't represent abstract value, this is exactly what happens. Prices are more likely to vary widely, and participants use the external, capitalist market to figure out how much labor hours are worth. In trying to remove the market from distribution, LETS just pushes it further into the background. When LETS schemes do succeed, they're often abandoned once local economies improve and members return to using regular money (understandably, since it's more widely exchangeable.) At this point, the scheme falls back on what Meeker–Lowry calls "the values of consciousness of its members." Once more, small groups of committed activists are supposed to substitute their own money and time for the global market.

Alternative currencies usually represent trading services–in–kind. They introduce time–lag: rather than using services immediately, participants can store what they have to trade in the community until another user comes along. However, these schemes don't work very well because they have to judge their worth against the existing, global market. 150 years ago, European labor exchanges attempted to bank and trade people's skills and goods. But there weren't enough goods when people needed them, and the system of goods allocation broke down. As we've seen, capitalism can't plan what's produced and distributed except according to imprecise market signals. On a smaller scale, that imprecision becomes more acute.

Money represents social production: it assigns values to commodities and allows the abstraction from concrete uses to take place. Money represents what Ingham calls a "promise to pay": to use it, everyone has to believe that his or her debts will be repaid. In that sense, economies are based on trust. But this isn't the same trust that localists invoke, as when Estill writes, "trade is a function of trust, and it is trusting one another that lies at the heart of our local economy." Rather, capital must trust states to enforce the right to accumulate, backed up by violence when necessary. A complex market needs an institution like a state to enforce general respect for property rights and one to generalize credit: a bank. Ingham points out that when Afghan warlords issue their own currency, they enforce the promise to pay better than the national state. Money represents the social and political aspects of capitalist power. Unfortunately, even the most ardent commitment to an alternative currency can't replace a global system of price signals.

This also applies to credit, money that banks issue to help future production. For localism, the power of shared trust and community can drive local banks to make low or no–interest loans to ethical businesses.

Historically, state or cooperative institutions have provided lower interest rates and better loans. But capitalism limits their potential for socially useful investment, particularly under globalization. Neoliberalism is defined by deregulating markets to attract capital, and even the recent cleanup of the American banking system has done little to change this dynamic. The importance of global, deregulated credit is best shown by its absence: in the financial crisis that began in 2008, banks stopped lending to each other, afraid of being burdened with bad debt. The credit system ground to a halt, and states poured trillions of dollars of public money into the banks to get credit flowing again. Banks expect capitalists to use credit to create new facilities they can't afford right now, generating surplus value and paying back interest. Banks have no desire to undermine that profitable lending relationship. Even those banks that do accept local currencies don't pay interest on them, for fear of paying more than market–based rates.

As long as acts of production are planned privately and separately, money is a necessary, abstract medium that represents those acts. This doesn't mean it's exclusive to capitalism. For example, feudal peasants made some goods for the market and exchanged them using currency. Credit also existed when peasants were indebted to their feudal masters and sharecroppers were indebted to landowners. But the point is that these forms weren't dominant. In a pre–capitalist economy, there were other tools of trade besides credit: peasants also exchanged goods directly. Under capitalism, people are dispossessed from the means of production, and have to sell their labor power to survive. Daily reproduction happens through the market. Direct exchange continues: some forms of it, such as unpaid domestic work, provide a source of free value for capital. But it's not the dominant way people survive: instead, money becomes the connecting link of all social–economic activity under capitalism.

The very fact that money is so central to exchange opens up political possibilities. The state can dictate financial system terms under which borrowing and lending takes place. With democratic pressure, the state could direct money towards socially useful ends, such as interest–free housing loans. In a socialist society, money could be a very different promise to pay: a medium that represents workers' portions of surplus labor. But for that to function, the supply and demand of commodities would have to be guaranteed from the outset, so that individual and average labor times were the same and there would be no pressure to corner or undercut production or distribution. Yet capitalists can't agree to produce and distribute the surplus according to democratic, socially–determined priorities, because this would eliminate profit. For democratic money to function properly, workers would have to end their separation from the means of production: in other words, to create socialism.

Right–wing localism: immigration

Marx called it "a pretty conception that – in order to reason away the contradictions of capitalist production – abstracts from its very basis and depicts it as a production aiming at the direct satisfaction of the consumption of the producers." Localism adopts this premise and assumes people have free choice to structure a capitalist economy. But when people make the wrong choices, then localism can become right-wing and anti–immigrant. It critiques globalization for strengthening multinational corporations at the expense of communities. But localism also applies the key neoclassical principle of scarcity to people, claiming we live in a world of infinite needs pursuing finite resources. It follows that self–sufficient communities won't need to invade other countries for their resources: moderate consumption will prevent the violence of large–scale trade. McKibben argues that in the face of fuel shortages, "a relatively self–sufficient county or state or region" will benefit "durable economies... (rather) than dynamic ones" by promoting community values and democracy. "Dynamic" is bad, "durable" is good. Schumacher uses an extended marine metaphor: "(n)ow, a great deal of structure has collapsed, and a country is like a big cargo ship in which the load is in no way secured. It tilts, and all the load slips over, and the ship founders." An idealization of the static ensues, in which "robust, local–scale economies" are "free of corporate manipulation, hidden subsidies, (and) waste."

A distrust of foreign people creeps in. Being rooted in a place enhances relationships, whereas "(m)obility erodes community." Migration brings displacement, alienation and excessive resource use. Describing a local arts scene (reliant on imported food and transplanted cultural industry workers), Estill suggests "it is entirely possible to be immersed in ideas, music, art, literature, and the stuff of culture without ever leaving town." This parochialism comes from a dislike of non–local workers, who don't contribute to local economies and spend what they earn elsewhere. Since value for localists is created only through exchange, foreign workers bring no benefit. Estill demands the end of commuting, refusing to hire non–locals.

Recognizing this streak of nativism, Libertarian Municipalism (LM) maintains a critical distance from localism. This isn't surprising since, of all localisms, it's most closely aligned to the revolutionary tradition. Biehl and Bookchin warn that small communities can become parochial, withdrawing "into themselves at the expense of wider consociation... A kind of municipal tribalism could spring up, one that shelters injustices or even tyrannies within."[7] They continue to defend smallness on the basis that State–led societies most often abuse human rights. However, localists are claiming the abuses of human conflict will stop, or at least lessen in local communities. If they create tyrannies as well, this is hardly a vision for the future.

Migration doesn't come from economies and countries "out of balance" as Schumacher contends. Workers must sell their labor power at the best possible price and move to do so. Capital moves too and moves first: cheaper labor power available abroad, saturated markets at home, the high costs of machine–production at home and barriers to capital export all force capital to seek lower–cost production facilities elsewhere. Workers follow the jobs. The disruption that this process causes helps capital in its heartlands, too: an estimated 5.3 million undocumented workers in the US come from countries where capital has displaced their communities. The agriculture and construction industries depend on that ill fortune. Absolute mobility for people is forbidden, yet workers have to move on capital's terms. Meanwhile land ownership, high rents and restrictive immigration policies all stop workers from leaving the labor market.

This process of dislocation isn't new. Schumacher finds historical precedents for localism in the self–sufficient commu- nities that existed in feudal Europe, where people were prohibited from migration by the high cost of transport, large–scale violence was uncommon and trade was restricted to luxuries. However, the link between violence and trade predates industrialism. Engels puts it at the beginning of class society, when rulers fought to control the social surplus. As we've seen, early Modern Europe's pre-capitalist, mercantilist economies focused on the slave trade. And it was small, rural English communities that ushered in capitalism by closing off common lands. In short, there's plenty of evidence of violence and trade in smaller, pre-industrial economies. By ignoring that history, Schumacher can link violence to trade and size, posing steady–state economies and static populations as the answer to impending scarcity.

He has no sympathy for workers drawn into large–scale migration. He castigates the "dependence on imports from afar and the consequent need to produce for export to unknown and distant peoples." The unknown peoples themselves are suspicious: "now everything and everybody has become mobile. All structures are threatened, and all structures are vulnerable to an extent that they have never been before." As McKibben warns, "how on earth do you grow at the rate the Chinese are growing, and not collapse?" The issue is not just China's very real ecological limits, but who takes responsibility for them: localism assumes that if people can choose what to consume, they can consume what and where to produce too. If they persist in desiring the Global North's standard of living, then it's their fault for being too greedy and consuming like us or moving next to us.

As an alternative, Schumacher proposes local industries for capital–poor regions, so people don't have to move to find work. McRobie takes this further, calling for small–scale manufacturing to develop rural industry. These aren't bad proposals: people stay rooted in particular places due to complex cultural, social and historical reasons, and an economy that met human needs would respect these choices instead of forcing workers to migrate. However, the point is that people should have a choice not only whether to leave, but over whether to stay. Not everyone wants to live on the land or work in small factories doing jobs that machines could do. This is, once again, a political question that localism doesn't address; instead, individuals trying to cope with the effects of capitalism become responsible for it.

This chapter suggests that localism sees capitalism as a market to trade things. The social relations of power disappear, and any remaining problems are technical. This lets pro–market localism portray capitalism as ethical and build small businesses that won't have to play by the rules of big capital. But small business isn't a check on capitalist development: it's another form of it. Small firms provide a vital, risk–taking function for capitalism as a whole, introducing new technologies and inhabiting margins of their own, opening ground for larger businesses. Even small firms must lower their costs by reducing the amount of value embodied in their commodities, leading to larger firms and often larger machines.

Anti–market localism suggests that we can replace big industry and high–tech to create a new, cooperative society based on direct, non–capitalist trade. But these plans are stymied by the law of value. By focusing on technical relations both pro– and anti–market localism miss the power of capital to dominate the market. Capital's inherent drives to profit expose local alternatives to ruthless market discipline. The contradiction between use and exchange–value production that drives capitalism into overproduction and crisis *begins* small and local.

Now we see the violence inherent in the system

By refusing to understand how capitalist goods are commodities first and use–values second, localists are stuck in the neoclassical paradigm, where individual property–owners exchange uses on the market. For Marx, this is more than just false: it "is accepting the present state of affairs; it is, in short, making an apology... for a society without understanding it." Unfortunately, any apology for capitalism gets in the way of finding real solutions. As Therborn points out, economists who accept the market always end up back where they began: at an ideal capitalism, with its ugly contradictions hidden behind visions of social harmony. This has a long history. John Stuart Mill, a supporter of Chartism, opposed working class political rule. Instead, he thought that class war could be avoided if workers formed cooperatives, getting their own capital and leaving the capitalists alone. Walras, a neoclassical economist, also supported cooperative commodity production as a way turn workers into small entrepreneurs. These economists were intent on preserving social peace from a fear of the poor challenging capitalist power.

Understanding this doesn't mean abstract theorizing: it poses historical, economic and political questions for those who say global capitalism can be transformed one small business at a time. Localism may not understand its own theory of value, but ironically this places it alongside Proudhon, who based his politics on an economy that had been marginalized by the middle of the nineteenth century. 150 years on and capital is bigger and more powerful than ever, yet localists are still calling for the same reforms, based on the same outmoded vision of capitalism. In fact, their schemes are a pale reflection of Proudhon's. He was attempting large–scale social engineering, trying to wrench the entire capitalist mode of production back to an earlier epoch. Localism has no such pretensions: in the face of oligopolies Proudhon could never have dreamt of in his worst nightmares, it creates tiny alternatives at the margins. In Proudhon's day, there were far more revolutionaries, their alternative schemes were far more numerous, and the capitalist system they were fighting was far weaker. The odds that localism's most cherished weapon of ethical commitment faced were far better than now. The consequences of this become clear when examining one of localism's favorite topics: urban agriculture.

Chapter Three

Growing Alternatives? Centralization, Rent and Agriculture

If there's one thing that most people associate with localist politics, it's urban agriculture (UA). Community gardens bring local residents and activists together to collectively produce food from urban plots. Community Supported Agriculture (CSA) allows consumers to purchase harvests directly from farmers in advance and receive produce throughout the year. Farmers' markets, buyers' coops, community kitchens and other distribution methods create spaces for community organizing and networking. Many people enjoy gardening as a hobby, but localism says it's more than a pleasant way to get your hands dirty: advocates say it can overcome malnutrition and provide a greener model to feed us all.[8]

Capitalism has created economies of scale in agriculture: hourly output of agriculture increased 12 times between 1950 and 2000, while food prices rose at half the rate of inflation. Since World War II, 70 percent of agricultural land in the mid–western United States has been transformed into large monoculture corn or soybean crops. Six agribusinesses control 98 percent of seed sales across the globe. Coupled with this concentration is also a genuine ecological crisis in large–scale agriculture. Industrial farming in general, and factory farms in particular, pollutes groundwater and surfaces, incubates antibiotic–resistant diseases, reduces biodiversity, increases water salinization and harms workers and animals.

The localist response to these degradations is to reverse growth and deindustrialize agriculture, "rejecting everything that is *unnatural*," as Petrini puts it. This includes eliminating monocultures, using local varieties of plants and animals and creating complex and sustainable production methods. Local food expert Wayne Roberts summarizes the localist argument for UA: the "common sense view that farming takes up too much scarce space to ever be practical in the city is just wrong. Many crops can be grown intensively and economically on small plots that can be found anywhere in the city. With the possible exception of land, the city is as close as can be to most of the inputs that farmers need." Crops can be grown economically on small urban plots. Farmers can trade directly with customers in the city. Individuals and communities can control and produce their own food supplies.

However, localist UA fails to understand the power of capital in a market economy. Echoing Proudhon, localists counter–pose artisanal production to a developed capitalist economy. But UA has to play by market rules as soon as it tries to sell its goods. This means it has to face the power of capital centralization and faces an extra barrier because it takes up land that, in cities, would otherwise be used more profitably. That means it has to generate not only profit for the farmer but rent for the landlord. Those combined pressures limit UA to filling market niches, not replacing large–scale agriculture.

Detroit provides a good example of rent pressures. Once the center of car manufacturing, Detroit has seen years of industrial decline. The urban population, once 1.9 million, is expected to shrink to 700,000. Whole neighborhoods have disappeared; 17,000 acres of urban land have been left vacant. The city now has the highest poverty and foreclosure rates in the US and one of the highest official unemployment rates of 27 percent. These circumstances have attracted Hantz Farms L.L.C., which plans to create the world's largest urban farm in east Detroit, paying $30 million to create a 50 acre plot to grow produce, generate electricity from methane and wind power and recycle bio–waste. It will use techniques derived from existing agribusiness: water–

and air–only greenhouses and trellised orchards to grow more in small spaces. CEO John Hantz, a multimillionaire fan of Ayn Rand, describes his project in neoclassical language: "We can't create opportunities, but we can create scarcity." Making land scarce drives its value up, but that's hard to do in a place like Detroit, where new properties keep being abandoned and land values keep dropping. If successful, Hantz expects the development to generate tourism and supplementary development. Costs have so far averaged $3,000 per acre and, to recoup his investment and make a profit, Hantz will not invest further unless given free land and special, lower–tax zoning.

Detroit is the best–case scenario for localism: it combines a declining but still substantial population, a lack of public or private sector development and cheap land. Where else would community gardens and alternative economies flourish, if not at the margins of an ex–industrial city? Many UA projects do exist: however, even here, Detroit can't escape the market. Hantz is buying land and then waiting until the prospects for exchange–value improve, and he's relying on public money to do it. This is not a community initiative: Hantz is a capitalist and expects to recoup his investments. If capital can command not only large–scale agriculture but even dictate the prospects for local agriculture, this is a clear sign that centralization and rent determine the size, longevity and uses of UA.

How capitalism transforms the land

Localists aren't the first to identify agricultural limits. As early as 1850, agricultural economists blamed long–distance trade for soil erosion and nutrient loss. Marx saw how concentrating and improving agricultural production also disrupted the process of soil renewal. Industrial agriculture made short–term gains at the expense of environmental sustainability, and in response Marx thought humanity had a long–term responsibility to take care of the earth. However, he also understood that agribusiness is the

natural outcome of capital in land, creating efficiencies of
and boosting market power. Roberts' "possible exceptic
land" structures all other use–values. So to understand
limits, we first need to examine how capital has transforme
land.

Schumacher argues, "human life can continue wit
industry, whereas it cannot continue without agriculture."
is a false dichotomy: capital treats agriculture as an industry
capital itself came from rural property relations. Pre–capi
agriculture operated according to strict rules of custon
Europe, tenant farmers on large feudal estates gave the l(
portion of their produce. They could consume or trade
remainder themselves. Capitalist social relations destroyed
system, starting with the land. Two trends took place simul
ously. First, English feudal lords began enclosing the lands
peasants had previously held in common. By creating l
estates, the owners eliminated the peasants' subsistence li
directly. Second, productivity increased, and a few small far
were able to grow enough to pay rent to the landowners
start small farms and workshops of their own. They
employed their newly dispossessed neighbors.

The vast majority of peasants lost their livelihoods and
forced into wage labor on the new, larger farms, or they
expelled from the countryside altogether and went to liv
cities. Well before large–scale industry existed, the landow
applied industrial principles to agriculture to feed their worl
increase productivity and intensify work. This process of
and exploitation *created* the capitalist economy: not only
agriculture become a separate branch of industry, the w
concept of countryside and city came into being: the r
became sparsely populated and the urban concentrated.
growth of cities pushed farmers to grow exclusively for t
vast new markets, breaking the old feudal division of labor.

The global market in commodities has dominated the g

completely for 150 years; it dominated agriculture for centuries longer. The destruction of local agriculture wasn't a byproduct of capitalist development but an essential condition. This history turns sustainable local agriculture from a matter of technical reorganization into a quixotic charge on the foundations of capitalism itself. For capital didn't just transform the land and move on: it continues to confront and overcome new barriers to production.

Capital confronts land as a natural resource that it can't make itself. This means capitalists often can't purchase contiguous plots, forcing intensive investment on what they already own. Often that investment begins with purchasing the land, livestock and hiring large numbers of workers first, rather than buying labor–saving factory technology. This makes agriculture more expensive, at least initially, than other industries. In order to attain average profit rates, capitalist farmers must adopt technology to reduce the area under cultivation.

Marx predicted that employment in agriculture would decline as capital replaced human labor with machinery to lower commodity prices, just like in any other industry. Over the last 30 years, the tiny percentage of agricultural workers in the Global North shrank even further. Meanwhile agricultural output jumped dramatically after World War II after the introduction of machines and chemical fertilizers. Net value added in agriculture began a dramatic, if fluctuating, climb in the late 1970s, around the same time American produce began to be dumped on the markets of the Global South. Agriculture in the Global North continues to be far more efficient: agricultural workers in the Global North add over 10 times the amount of value as workers in the Global South. There, workers use ten times fewer numbers of machines. The Global South, still largely reliant on small–scale agriculture, does not generate the same productivity or efficiency as the Global North. Even if it was desirable to recreate an economy of small farmers, it would mean reversing long–term

historical trends towards capital centralization, imperialist trade relations and occupational and demographic shifts that have been firmly established for decades.

In a factory, capital can introduce new machinery to streamline manufacturing and increase productivity. However, agriculture presents special problems. Capital can only profit by circulating through the M–C–M′ process as quickly as possible, yet it can't speed up the seasons. Other industries can make products all year round; to achieve similar profit levels, agribusiness needs to do the same. Capital introduces machines for faster processing, but those machines must operate constantly to pay for themselves. This encourages more intensive production on highly capitalized plots. This is the source of factory farms, which produce far more on single plots than small, poorly–funded farms do. The size of land under culti-vation shrinks overall, but the size of individual farms grows. The result of this process is cheaper production on large indus-trial farms. These changes increased output per acre by 150 percent and output per worker by 210 percent from the late 1930s to the mid–1960s. Today's low prices for food show how success-fully capital has applied mechanization to reduce the value of food commodities, in order to sell more of them.

The intense pressure to overcome natural limits means that capital centralization is *higher* in agriculture than in other indus-tries, which restricts capitalist farming to bigger firms. The size of farms and ownership continues to grow: for example, in 1920, farms over 1,000 acres used 33 percent of American land; this proportion had increased to 60 percent by 1959. The number of farms over 1,000 acres grew by 14 percent between 1982 and 2002. Small farms are disappearing across Europe: France lost half its farmers between 1982 and 1999, while Germany experi-enced a 25 percent loss in the 1990s. The US has lost two thirds of its farms since 1920, while only 2 percent of Americans still live on farms. Large farms produce more efficient output: yet as output goes up, prices fall and farms need to become even bigger to realize a profit. Growth is self–reinforcing: the bigger the output, the more land and machinery is needed to produce it. Processing creates more value than raw material production, and agribusinesses are able to capture many points of the commodity chain that small farmers can't.

The growth of ownership and farm sizes are tendencies. Small farms, of course, continue to exist. Just like other small businesses, they perform useful services to capital, taking on many risks that large firms would rather avoid such as operating with smaller profit margins. Big capital doesn't have to control everything directly: as long as small farms are indebted, big capital can set the conditions under which production takes place. Owner–occupiers are reduced to supervisors and receive a small share of any value produced. Those small farmers who can't produce efficiently enough lose their farms.

Agribusinesses can produce horrendous externalities: for example, 2009's swine flu epidemic is said to have come from a poorly–managed hog factory farm. But the ecological benefits of small farming depend on specific circumstances. Conventional crops fix more nitrogen than organic ones, while there are no differences in nutritional value between conventional and organic produce. Even with large–scale agriculture, the environmental impact isn't always as severe as localist literature contends, and the impact of small–scale farming on energy use and land conservation is complex[9]

Capital's drive for exchange–value puts up three major barriers to small–scale farming. First, agriculture was enmeshed in capitalism even before industry was. Second, capital tries to overcome land's natural barriers to production by applying technology intensively. Usually, very small areas can't produce enough to generate average profits, but Hantz Farms' example may disprove this. Third, larger farms continue to grow in size and market share. Big capital either takes over smaller capitals directly or lets them self–manage under severe credit constraints. Small farms that manage to maintain themselves help, not hinder, capital centralization.

What is rent?

Rent emerges from one of the more obscure corners of Marxist theory.[10] It shows how exchange–value, not use–value, determines land use in capitalism. When landlords own the land where production takes place, producers have to pay them to use it. Rent was a big concern for the early industrial bourgeoisie, locked in struggle with the land–owning aristocracy. Classical political economy, the bourgeoisie's intellectual cudgel, had to show why the aristocracy no longer mattered. If labor created all wealth, as Ricardo said, then landlords were parasites who just skimmed off a portion of the total, diverting otherwise productive investment.

Marx took this analysis further, rooting rent in the social relations of capitalism. He saw that some land is such poor quality that it's too expensive to produce on. But since food was a necessity, food grown on poor land could still be sold. The worst quality land that could still make a profit generated *absolute rent* for landlords. Production on better land cost less and generated more surplus: this created *differential rent*.

In a factory, the capitalist with the newest machines makes and sells more goods. It's the same with land. Tenants with more capital can increase the productivity of the land, lower the prices of their commodities and get higher–than–average profits, at least until the landlord raises the rent. Two conclusions apply. First, rent isn't just a stolen portion of surplus value, as Ricardo thought. Landlords who own the land and demand payment for its use create a social barrier to capital. Their presence forces capitalists to innovate, generating higher profits to make rent a smaller portion of their costs. Second, and more centrally for localism, size matters: capitalists attempt to overcome natural barriers to production by applying more capital. Any theory supporting UA must begin with how large capital has a social advantage over small capitals, since it can make more drastic improvements to the land.

Rent today

Capital tries to eliminate all its obstacles; if capital could eliminate landed property, rent would disappear as well. In most parts of the world, the aristocracy doesn't exist anymore, but rent does. This suggests we still need it as a theoretical tool, to explain how capitalist ownership changes land in general and UA in particular.

Rent isn't just a drain on capitalist finances. It determines what gets produced and how much capital gets invested in a particular space. It equalizes profits between agriculture and other sectors, so that capital doesn't rush into agriculture to earn super–profits and spark a crisis of overproduction. Rent centralizes capital by taking income from many small farmers. By taxing profits, rent forces producers to introduce new technologies and change the landscape: for example, factory farms concentrate production in one place to avoid the costs of renting large tracts of land. Those farms may visit unmitigated horrors on workers and animals, but their purpose for capital is to circumvent older forms of property. This development, in turn, leads to agribusinesses that smaller capitals can't create on their own. Rent coordinates capital through a push–pull relationship. Landowners bring land on the market to *achieve* rents. Agricultural capitalists invest in new technologies to *avoid* rent.

In a developed capitalist economy, it doesn't matter whether farmers are tenants or own their own land. Everyone still has to achieve SNALT. Tenant farmers have to earn enough to pay rent to landowners, while owners take out bank loans to make technical improvements, for which they owe interest. If owners refuse to take out loans, their rent is the income lost from refusing to develop their land, risking being driven under by more efficient producers.

Today's owners aren't the decadent landlords of the aristocracy, using up profits on extravagant tastes rather than investing in production. As capitalism developed, landlords found themselves with rents that could be invested for even greater returns. This surplus capital funded the first banks, turning landlords into financiers and transforming them into another fraction of the capitalist class. Rent was the midwife to capitalism, helping individual capitals to centralize. Today, landed property and industrial capital are simply two different ways to generate more capital: there are no separate class interests between landowners and production owners. For Marx, farmers were capitalists who produce commodities from the land rather than factories. This is even truer today.

Rent also helps describe how capital accumulation works through space. Capitalists compete for the best location in terms of land price, infrastructure, distance to market and so on. Industrial capitalists earn more surplus value from improving production technology; agricultural capitalists can do the same, as well as earning higher profits from better locations.

This discussion only does cursory justice to a complex, decades–old debate, but we can summarize a few principles. The use–values of land don't exist on their own: like the use–values of any commodity, they're created by the struggle of capital to exploit labor. Capital needs workers in agriculture like it needs workers in factories and offices. Capitalists only realize a profit if they can sell the use–values contained in commodities according to global market prices, raising output to undersell competitors; since capital doesn't eat, this creates intense pressure to internationalize markets or convert agricultural goods into non–foodstuffs like ethanol. To lower wages and increase output, capital subjects land to factory–style efficiencies. Yet as long as locational, social and technological advantages in certain spaces remain, the resulting surplus can be appropriated as rent. The needs of capital accumulation and the market in land determine land use, not the needs of people.

Exchange– and use–value frame localist UA. It must compete with capital's constant production and transport improvements. But if it does so successfully and generates surplus profits, landowners will levy higher rents. This puts localist UA in a bind. In particular circumstances, with enough investment and subsidies, UA can succeed as a capitalist business. The same can't be said for anti–market UA that produces use–values: as soon as land values rise, differential rents do too and more profitable land uses take over.

Pro–market urban agriculture

Capitalist agriculture has to make a profit. Any excess profits are skimmed off as rent, which is determined by the costs of producing on marginal land. If producers improve the land, the rent goes up. However, unlike rural agriculture, UA faces this challenge from all land uses in the city, not just other growers. In other words, if more rent can be generated from industry, housing or infrastructure, UA will lose out. Some urban farmers have recognized this and aim to beat big agribusiness at its own game.

Agribusiness's biggest problem is reducing the space between production and consumption. This gives UA one main advantage: it's closer to urban markets and saves on trans-portation costs. For–profit small, urban farms combine their location benefits with cost–savings from free friend and family labor, replacing farm workers. By using intensive cropping and urban greenhouses to create high–volume production, these farms can also create space for spin–off businesses like food preparation and compost generation. These initiatives have had some success: while the number of American middle–sized farms is decreasing, the number of small farms, defined as 50 acres or less, has risen by around 17 percent between 1982 and 2007. However, small farms account for only two percent of farmland, while farms over 1,000 acres cultivate two thirds. Both small farms and those over 2,000 acres have grown. This suggests that, while capital centralization in agriculture continues, profit–seeking UA can fill market niches. However, there's no information as to whether these new US small farms are rural or urban. Agribusiness can apply its capital to reduce the time and cost of bringing goods to market. If higher rents and profits can be generated through other uses, urban farms will not be able to compete and farmers will resist their introduction, as the following examples show.

The Markham Foodbelt

Municipal planners have tried to encourage UA by zoning for a foodbelt: land in or near city boundaries reserved for food production. Markham, a municipality north of Toronto, Ontario, proposed reserving 60 percent of its boundaries for limited population growth and intensified development, while preserving the remaining 40 percent of agricultural land and wilderness. The proposal planned to protect agricultural jobs, promote local food, stop suburban sprawl and preserve the watershed.

However, the local farmers' business group opposed the development freeze. It meant existing land values would rise, making renting farmland prohibitive. There would be no incentive to improve their farmland, since any returns from capital investment would be eaten up by higher mortgages. One farmer denounced a development freeze by stating, "You are taking a free–market situation and you are legislating something... that's going to devalue the land. That's communism." If communism meant blocking market access, the farmers were right: they wanted to take advantage of rising differential rents on their plots. They also denounced the localist alternatives of craft production and agritourism, since large–scale agriculture generates higher rents than smaller–scale ventures. Markham farmers compete with produce from across the globe and, as one farmer put it, "We are never going to be the lowest–cost crop producer, ever, in the world." The city councillor who proposed the freeze blamed "vested interests" on farmer opposition. Meanwhile 83 percent support of Markham residents supported the foodbelt. The undoubtedly genuine enthusiasm for local produce and green space may also have had a parochial side: the anti–development campaign was pitched as explicitly anti–growth, warning about "damage to community values and existing property values." Eventually, the demands of the farmer–capitalists for growth defeated the Food Belt initiative at a city council vote.

The foodbelt proposal pitted citizens who wanted community–oriented use–values against a range of capitalist interests. Farmers feared restrictions on their ability to expand into new land. The banks and developers saw a chance to profit from different land–uses. The entire agro–food sector in Markham generated $62 million in revenue from 6,617 hectares of farmland in 2006, while developers paid $100 million for a single, 204–hectare farm in 2009. The math is clear: Markham generated $9,369 per hectare for farming, while the farm in question generated $490,196 per hectare for housing. Put differently, that single farm generated 52 times higher differential rents, 'improving' the land by changing its use altogether. Who wouldn't sell out?

Capitalists also aren't above using UA to lower their own rent. The city of Vancouver allowed developers to reclassify vacant lots from commercial use to parkland, lowering their property taxes by 70 percent. In some cases this meant planting a few trees on lots next to highways, in others it meant creating community gardens. Omni Developers saved over $2 million; one property worth $24 million had its tax cut by $357,000 per year. Prima

Properties Inc. saved $345,000 on another $24 million plot. Local non-profit, the Vancouver Public Space Network, even partnered with Prima to allocate new community garden spaces. According to one columnist, taxpayer subsidies to community gardens, determined by lost tax revenue from corporations, amounted to $350 per tomato plant. When a recent Vancouver development incorporated the existing community garden into the condo design, it didn't generate rent through production; instead, the garden helped raise rents for future uses and generate subsidies from a credulous city government.

Capitalist farmers won't upgrade land if new profits get siphoned off as rent; however, when landowners treat land as a financial asset, speculative capital can step in to intensify or change land-use. This can create an alliance between capitalist and landowner, or in Markham's case between farmer and developer, both acknowledging that higher rents from housing vastly outweigh the profit from farming. The local state can encourage local farms, but it also has to plan land use to reflect higher values. The development industry is a powerful lobby and, like all corporate entities, can shape tax policy. More fundamentally, the state won't readily undermine private property by interfering with profitable land markets, as the farmers feared. Reflecting these tensions, Markham was the only municipality in the region to even consider limiting growth. The foodbelt battle shows that capital tries to impose its interests on all its different sectors: farmers, banks and developers.

Anti-market urban agriculture

These examples don't mean that businesses will win every battle over land use. But rent sets strict limits on what's possible. Markham's plan encouraged for-profit UA, yet it didn't generate prospective rents high enough to satisfy capital. It follows that non-profit UA, dedicated to providing use-values, faces an even tougher battle.

There are plenty of benefits to UA. It uses land more intensively, grows more diverse products, recycles bio–waste and, by
reducing transportation costs, lowers energy usage and carbon
emissions. People get healthy food, physical exercise, education,
job skills, a small income and community safety. Most localists
don't claim UA is revolutionary; McKibben argues that gardening
reduces "hyper–individualism" but "(i)t *doesn't* require that you
join a commune or become a socialist." However, UA can change
you personally: even shopping at a farmers' market "begins to
build a different reality ... (that) responds to all the parts of who
we are." Carrlson claims that UA allows "gardeners ... to
refashion their lives in tune with their own visions, know–how,
and multidimensionality." Like Fourier, who promoted
gardening as a form of "attractive labor," gardens can prefigure a
post–capitalist society. They encourage collaboration, "sharing
tools, land, knowledge, labor, customers, and money" in a
democratic structure that provides "land tenure, food security,
and economic survival." Put together, local UA groups create
what Roberts calls a "cohesive food movement" that is the
natural heir to the labor, women's and democracy movements.

Community gardens have a long history in the US. The
government promoted them in World Wars I and II and the
Depression, involving millions of families. Gardening lost
popularity as post–war incomes increased and agriculture industrialized, but garden spaces increased during the municipal
bankruptcies of the 1970s when the number of vacant lots rose.
With the extra land and federal funds, community gardens fed
200,000 residents by 1980 and grew $17 million worth of produce
in 1982. However, President Reagan capped funding for
community gardens and it ended entirely in 1992. Some
government–supported local food programs continue, but many
garden advocates have turned to private or municipal funds.

Poor people pay 30 percent of their disposable income for
food, which is more than double the average. They also live in

"food deserts", neighborhoods without supermarkets. In response, UA advocates try to redress poverty, inequality and malnutrition by building Community Food Security (CFS), which uses the provision of healthy, sustainably grown food to address broader inequalities. For example, community gardens can build CFS by providing produce for local cooking classes, which in turn build the job skills of poor people. Participants can connect with each other outside the market through volunteer farm labor, part of what Roberts calls "giving the poor 'a hand up rather than a hand–out'." Governments can support CFS by including food in community planning, purchasing local produce for schools and zoning for quality supermarkets. Public health authorities have conducted studies showing positive health outcomes for a range of food security programs.

It's absolutely true that UA can provide healthy food to a small number of poor people who can't get fresh vegetables otherwise. However, existing assessments look at individual projects: there are no broad impact studies. On the one hand, this is just a matter of resources: so many factors contribute to health, including diet, food access and employment that it's hard for a cash–strapped community group to measure success. But the problem goes deeper: these programs don't take into account the power of agribusiness to dominate the market and produce cheap commodities. An alternative could be fighting for the regulation and nationalization of food production and super-markets and setting price controls, but that would interfere with property rights. Rather, UA advocates want to make the market more accessible. Provide poor people with ways to grow food and learn new skills, and they'll get jobs and health. Market justice will prevail, just like Proudhon said.

However, distribution measures face high food costs and land values. In Toronto, Ontario, almost all farmers' markets are located outside of poor neighborhoods. Good Food Box programs can supply produce directly from farmers to people living in food deserts, but the Boxes are expensive for people on fixed incomes. In social housing, they face an added barrier because poor tenants associate the boxes' delivery with rent collection. Although early data suggested most Good Food Box consumers were low income, the very poorest are excluded. Small markets have a lower mark–up than supermarkets and a not–for–profit status, but they still require subsidies to exist. Farmers' markets, supposed to provide CFS for poor consumers, charge higher prices simply because small–scale production and distribution are more expensive.

UA advocates are aware of these problems and demand anti–poverty measures, but they're often posed alongside community garden initiatives, as if gardens can make up for a lack of income. However, the problem is poverty, not access to markets. Food security comes from income security, something UA was never meant to address. In the only study so far to examine how localist UA affects low–income food security, the use of community gardens and kitchens by poor people was "so low that we could not even analyze the relationship between community garden or kitchen participation and household food insecurity."[11] This makes sense, as local food requires huge amounts of resources and labor, including harvest, transport and other tasks. Across Canada, the "participation of low–income households in food charity programs nationally is also low."

In fact, poor people are the *least* likely to have the money, vehicles and tools needed to grow their own food and shop in the right places. Yet localist projects still have a popular, CFS–friendly image. In their defense, Friendly argues that individual UA programs "are measured against a vast set of systemic roots of food insecurity, which no isolated local program alone can counteract." This may not be an accident, because actual government support for CFS is meager, and funding for initiatives is often on a once–only, individual project basis. By providing occasional funding to community gardens, governments can claim to be addressing food security. Promoting CFS risks letting government off the hook for refusing to address poverty directly. There's an ethical issue as well: being poor is already expensive and time–consuming, so why should poor people be forced to work more just to be healthy?

The impact of rent

Gardens provide social, economic and health benefits for gardeners. However, improving the neighborhood raises land values, which means that sustaining urban gardens can lead to their own demolition. Community gardens must either be insulated from the law of value through subsidies or generate sufficient rents.

For example, Detroit has over 900 community gardens, mostly under a quarter of an acre, which grow produce for use, not the market. However, Hantz's Farm has alarmed CFS advocates who fear a land grab that could push their own not–for–profit gardens out. Later phases could include expanding the farm to 20,000 acres to grow non–food crops like Christmas trees. If Hantz can overcome the technical barriers, farming relatively small areas of land can be profitable. Farming on small–*owned* plots is not. This doesn't matter when people just want to grow their own food, but what happens when the capitalists muscle in? Marx wrote of an English landowner who moved to the Australian outback with 1,500 workers, who all promptly left the farm and vanished into the wilderness. Enough free land was available that the landowning capitalist couldn't exclude others from it. But by encouraging scarcity in land, applying capital to it and even stealing techniques from use–value UA, Hantz can both push out small and not–for–profit owners and generate differential rent.

The South Central Urban Farm shows how much attention the market pays to differential rent. In 1994, the Los Angeles municipality granted temporary use of an urban 14–acre plot to

the LA Regional Food Bank. Latin American immigrants culti-
vated small gardens and managed the land democratically. In
2003, former landlord Horowitz sued the city to regain
ownership and was offered the property for $5 million. The city
began serving eviction notices on the farmers in 2004, leading
them to occupy the farm. With help from a national non–profit
and celebrities, the Farm raised $16 million to meet Horowitz's
asking price. However, after an initial endorsement, Horowitz
requested two million more and finally refused the deal. In
addition to Horowitz's personal dislike for the activists, the
squatters wouldn't compensate him for land that had appreciated
in value, ignoring the differential rents that he felt he was owed.
Within the farmers' movement, some also opposed granting the
farmers permanent tenure, fearing that legalized squatting
would discourage other landowners from issuing temporary
land–use permits. Horowitz was happy to provide other
use–values for the land if he could get a decent price for it.

These conflicts emerge when localists attempt to commodify
land–use, turning their socially–useful services into sellable
goods. For example, when poor farmers produce use–values like
carbon–storage, water purification and animal habitats, they
generate an estimated three trillion dollars per year of services to
the global ecosphere. The World Bank suggests paying for land's
environmental services. However, by attaching a price tag to
those eco–services, commodifying land would actually increase
differential rents. This would lead to massive estates of
landowners who could speculate on the new values of their land.
Government would have to raise taxes to pay for these new rents.
The only way to make environmental services truly free is for
government to expropriate the land, as in Cuba, calling into
question property rights as a whole.

Urban agriculture in the Global South
This book only touches on the Global South, because its

economies are vastly different from the North's. However, since localists often suggest subsistence farming provides a model for a sustainable economy, it's worth examining how capital transforms agriculture everywhere.[12]

There are real use–values in agro–ecology and non–industrial production of forest, sea, meadow and insect resources in the Global South. Yet if agro–ecology could generate rent, even insect farms would be commodified, centralizing land ownership and dispossessing peasants. Common land would disappear and, as numerous Marxists have pointed out, this has been a vital part of capitalist growth from seventeenth century England to today. Agribusiness has opened up the markets of the Global South, subjecting food prices to the same volatility as all commodities and creating hunger and malnutrition among the world's poor.

This has little to do with a lack of food or resources to produce it. For example, agribusiness uses oil for cultivation and transport, and some commentators have linked current high food prices to the high cost of oil. However, food prices are also rising because of profit and geopolitics: in a quest for stable domestic energy supplies, and as a form of subsidy to large grain producers, the EU and US have switched 12 percent of world maize production to biofuels. Speculators used this market–imposed scarcity to drive food prices up in the late 2000s. After a decline, prices rose again: by January 2011 the UN's food price index, an aggregate cost of six staple goods, was the highest since records began in 1990. This time commentators blamed unpredictable weather, but the underlying problem was that traders gambled on the predicted scarcity of supply to drive prices up and make a profit.

When capital in the Global North invests in land, outputs rise and food is overproduced, meaning commodities can't be sold profitably at home. But subsidies mean that even poor–quality lands in the North can still earn rents in the South or, as with biofuels, create entirely new commodities. With worse–quality land brought into production, higher rent becomes available, fuelling more overproduction. These high rents don't just earn money for agribusiness: by driving out smaller, less efficient competitors, they can force open markets to capital. Combined with the neoliberal political project, dumping subsidized produce clears land for producing cash crops for the world market on a rationalized, large–scale basis, starting the cycle of overproduction again. Ernest Mandel calls this the "permanent crisis" of agriculture. Future rents, and not the use–value of food or oil, sets prices. This means that small–scale production isn't permanently viable in the Global South either.

Cuba

McKibben suggests that use–value UA is can be scaled upwards; despite disavowing socialism, he cites Cuba as a successful example of large–scale organic gardening. In the early 1990s, the USSR collapsed and Cuba lost its Soviet subsidies and trade. Lacking oil to power its farm machinery, famine loomed and Cuba entered its Special Period. It wasn't more expensive to pay for industrial agriculture, it was impossible: the source of oil and capital–intensive machinery simply disappeared. This kind of *deus ex machina* delights localists who rely on the peak oil thesis to predict the growth of small–scale production. As Roberts says, "Cuba–type scenarios (will) become more common in a world of increasing climate chaos and resource scarcity." However, stripped of its emotive appeal, Cuban UA was a response to crisis: for its political survival, the Cuban regime had to find new sources of nutrition and created moral incentives to justify the material sacrifice food the Special Period required. The state switched 400,000 hectares of sugar production to other foods, creating free or low–cost meals at schools and workplaces. Community gardening rose to prominence, as urban vegetable production tripled and urban gardens filled 12 percent of

Havana. The city farms created numerous benefits, alleviating unemployment, eliminating the costs of transport and storage and providing urban wastes for fertilizer.

However, the Cuban example would be hard to repeat. Normally, capital substitutes machines for human labor to drive down costs. Cuba did the opposite; but since the state controls the land and labor markets and appropriates rent, it could choose a less–efficient form of cultivation and still maintain lower prices. No free market would allow this level of state intervention, but Cuba shows what a command economy not dictated by rent pressures could accomplish. Agricultural land is divided between state–controlled plots and cooperatives, which combine aspects of private and collective land ownership. Cuba allows some farmers' markets, but the Ministry of Agriculture sets maximum prices. Cooperatives have titles to the land, but the farms must contain members of the Communist Party and sell produce at officially designated markets.

Cuba also faces severe external constraints. It's blockaded; in fact, the community gardening policy arose out of military strategy, as Cuba planned for a long–term occupation by foreign powers and wanted its citizen–soldiers to be self–sufficient. Its political and economic isolation allowed the Cuban state to determine land use, according to the need to grow food or get foreign currency. In this respect, Havana's urban gardens represent a kind of differential rent: capital applied intensively to the same small plots of land, improving it and allowing the state to reap the benefits. It remains to be seen whether economic liberalization will allow this kind of non–market production to continue. In an economy with a market in land, a high population density and a capitalist democracy, urban farmland would be subject to speculation.

UA advocates suggest a city like Toronto could grow 10 percent of its fresh produce within its own borders. However, like most of the Global North, Toronto doesn't have a pool of unemployed agricultural workers. Cuba employs 10 people per hectare in agriculture, 300,000 people out of a population of 11 million. This is far more intensive than in the US or Canada: mass unemployment and 'inefficient' labor is something poor countries have in abundance. Roberts acknowledges "profound differences in the ecology, crops, food production methods and people's history of countries in the Global South and North." However, except for the latter, these are mainly technical concerns; from a Marxist perspective, they reflect whether capital directly owns agricultural production or lets small producers do it. Either way, capital remains in control and pressures farmers to keep prices below market averages.

Finally, localists are remarkably flexible about the scale of their analysis. In 2007, Malawi purchased fertilizer to triple yields rather than buying emergency aid. Roberts calls this "local self–reliance and self–rule in food matters... rather than placing authority in institutions and markets far from the scene." Yet the output was still sold on the world market to generate revenue. Localism stretches to include Cuban national policy, ISI and the Malawian government, inserted into a chain of global commodity production. The criticism of size disappears and a straight-forward Keynesian state intervention remains, subject to the dangers of inflation and debt–financing of all Keynesian projects.

It is hard to see how these conditions, specific to the political economy of the Global South, could happen in the Global North short of massive state intervention, something localists themselves would condemn as Modernist and industrialist. The only other government making organic farming official policy is Hamas in the Gaza Strip; also facing international isolation, it's unable to obtain fertilizer or machinery due to the Israeli blockade but has yet to attract localist attention. The popular upheavals of 2011 in the Middle East arose in part from higher food prices, showing that revolution, and not subsistence gardening, is another possible outcome to the crisis of agriculture in the Global South.

Urban agriculture as resistance?

To sum up, capital centralizes land ownership to try to produce more and drive down costs. This creates surplus capital that, in turn, drives more centralization and creates higher rents. Agribusiness dominates food production because of its advantages in technology, economies of scale and political weight. In specific circumstances, pro– and anti–market UA can create niche markets or provide use–values. But both have to confront capitalist competition.

UA must earn differential rent, since it's located in cities where plenty of rent is available from other uses. Even when a city is deindustrializing, like Detroit, rent's absence can signal future new land uses for capital. If higher rents are available through real estate speculation, owners will resist UA, as the examples of Markham, Los Angeles and other cities demonstrate. This relationship has even been institutionalized: for example, the UK government's Food 2030 program proposed temporary community gardens, with leases that can be cancelled when land values increase. Subsidies distort this process further, keeping poor quality land in production.

Profit–seeking UA may generate higher rents, but the benefits are temporary as capital subjects agriculture to the same pressures of mechanization like any other industry. When agribusiness uses technology to replace humans, it can drive down commodity costs to the point where UA's lower transportation costs don't give it any competitive edge. And since small farms are more likely to be mortgaged, any higher rents they generate will go right back to the bank. Consumers can subsidize UA, but this isn't a long–term basis for scaling up or sustaining local production.

Could large–scale farming be environmentally benign? It would certainly be very expensive to clean up run–off and, if land lay fallow to regenerate sufficiently, this would create far larger farms. Hantz's farm and recent buzz about multi–story urban farm towers suggests that, once again, capital can use technology to overcome these obstacles and even reduce waste. It can find ways to use heavy machinery in small spaces and avoid expensive rents by building up rather than out.

There are alternatives to mono–cropping and factory farms. Agro–ecology incorporates both small and large–scale farming, while organic farming adapts to landscapes rather than imposing monocultures, leading Joel Kovel to call them "highly developed (forms of) social production" which have the potential to be anti–capitalist. But until the local food movement strategizes how to confront capital's power, it's unlikely agro–ecology will be adopted on a large scale. As long as ecological alternatives depend on building micro–alternatives, capital will prevail. As Robin Murray argues, "Any reforms... to establish a poorly capitalized, independent small farmer class as the backbone of productive agriculture, is already archaic and will be treated by history as such."

Rent–to–own

Some CFS advocates recognize that small–business and activist DIY can't create food security and call for food politics to become part of overall urban policy. In the meantime, providing access to growing cheap, nutritious food can help workers lower their cost of living by surviving outside the market. Frederich Engels, in his pamphlet *The Housing Question,* suggested the question was more complex. Reforms like cheaper rent, transit and even community gardens can make it cheaper for workers to live, but they also allow capitalists to lower wages. Even when workers are free from direct rent, they still have to pay.

However, some suggest the logic of rent follows capital too closely. Workers are allowed to produce surplus value but have no impact on distributing it; capital takes market share while workers don't. In fact, life outside the market is a way for workers, not just banks or landlords, to earn rent. By providing a better quality of life, small measures can give workers the means to organize politically to fight for reforms. As Steven Katz argues, when "workers struggle to impose their own price on shelter and space, and their own meanings on land; when they refuse to permit their spaces to be used for the reproduction of capital; and when they struggle collectively to define their communities and cities as self–organized spatial use–values, these are forms of the struggle for workers' rent."[13] Carrlson suggests CFS is part of that struggle and that small projects can agglomerate and overcome the capitalist system. This subversion is not only anti–capitalist but non–capitalist: by surviving outside the market, people could use UA to eventually separate themselves completely. If this is true, then paying too much attention to centralization and rent cuts off the possibility of resistance.

However, workers don't have much of a choice about what their spaces get used for. Their existence as *workers* means that they absorb costs for capital just by doing what they need to survive: non–market activities like cooking, cleaning and maintaining a house save capital the cost of providing those services. UA can spark community organizing because many projects include an important educational role, but it can just as easily spark tedium and frustration, both because it's being done for survival and because activists have to spend their time defending themselves from rent–seeking capitalists. The possibilities of resistance come from existing political conditions, and the last 30 years of neoliberalism suggest that workers haven't clawed much rent back recently. UA can provide vital spaces to create collective consciousness, and this is ultimately a subjective question that depends on the concrete circumstances of each project. However, this chapter has argued that UA's prospects for creating successful projects that move beyond friendly local spaces to challenge the market are slim. Too many experiences of defeat can damage hopes for building a more ecologically healthy world.

While it's important to celebrate the fact that people find ways to survive by any means necessary, an equally important question is what people do to resist, and this poses strategic political questions. Before we can discuss resistance, however, we have to take a step back and consider the appeal of alternatives. If localism has little impact apart from marginal projects, why is it so popular? The answer lies in a complex mix of the pessimism, utopianism, and life expectations of the localists themselves. In a word, localism is an ideology.

Chapter Four

Local Shops for Local People

In *The Road to Wigan Pier*, George Orwell wondered why socialism was so unpopular, when democratic economic planning could alleviate the Great Depression's mass unemployment. He ended up blaming the socialists themselves. The socialist "proposes to level the working class 'up' (up to his own standard) by means of hygiene, fruit–juice, birth–control, poetry, etc." Promoting lifestyles, combined with snobbery and eccentricity, separated socialists from the vast majority of people. Revolution didn't "mean a movement of the masses with which they hope to associate themselves" but "a set of reforms which 'we', the clever ones, are going to impose upon 'them', the Lower Orders." These moralists were drawn "entirely from the middle class, and from a rootless town–bred section of the middle class at that," forming a "dreary tribe of high–minded women and sandal–wearers and bearded fruit–juice drinkers who come flocking towards the smell of 'progress' like blue–bottles to a dead cat." Their socialism was not freedom but a "dictatorship of the prigs."[14]

Socialism means the working class organizing society to meet its own needs. But there's another, more common version: socialism 'from above', in which, as Hal Draper describes it, "(s)ocialism (or "freedom," or what–have–you) is to be handed down, in order to Do the People Good, by the rich and powerful out of the kindness of their hearts." Engels saw it as a contract: the rich could donate a small portion of their income to charity, in order not to be confronted by capitalism's worst effects. But it followed that the poor had to behave themselves, reforming their individual behavior rather than organizing collectively to overthrow capitalism. From this arose a class–based prejudice against "rambunctious" lifestyles, which localism shares.

For example, take Kingsolver's argument that poor people can enjoy healthy food providing they change their "attitude" to exercise "patience and a pinch of restraint – virtues that are hardly properties of the wealthy." Hygiene and poetry have been replaced by ethical consumption and Do–It–Yourself, but the high–mindedness of patience and restraint remains. Orwell tells of "Society dames (who) now have the cheek to walk into East End houses and give shopping–lessons to the wives of the unemployed…. First you condemn a family to live on thirty shillings a week, and then you have the damned impertinence to tell them how they are to spend their money." How come the middle class socialists of Orwell's day, and the localists of today, are so concerned with how individuals act? The answer lies in ideology.

What ideology does

Ideology often means a fancy way of saying someone's wrong: you have the facts, they have ideology. But it's far more than that. Ideas don't come from nowhere: they're shaped by how we live in a class–divided society.

Unfortunately, this can lead to a stereotypical view of ideology. If our ideas come from classes, then external structures dictate what we think: workers think a certain way, rulers think another way and we have no free will of our own. Of course it's not that simple: there's no automatic link between what we do for a living and the ideas in our heads. To understand this, we have to delve into how the division of labor works and how it structures ideas.[15]

According to Marx, what defines humans is how we act creatively, producing ourselves, others and society. Precisely because these are activities, they vary. The social division of labor describes people as they relate to each other, socially and economically, in an ever–changing process of production and reproduction.

Sociologists often use the phrase 'class position', fixing classes as points on a graph. However, class needs to be understood first as a *relation* to the mode of production: at its simplest level, whether we own capital or work for a living.

Since classes experience the division of labor very differently, their perception of exploitation is also very different. In turn, a class's understandings create meaning that people act on to shape the world. But class and ideology don't match directly: they're mediated by historical factors and social context. As Raymond Williams suggests, ideology is a field of contested meanings, some of which are free–floating, while others line up more closely with ruling powers.

If workers are so exploited, how come they believe in capitalist ideology? In a phrase: commodity fetishism. Relations between things stand in for relations between people: the impersonal market moves goods around while we watch it happen and try to survive as individuals, jumping at the chance to sell our labor power. Powerlessness and selfishness are a result: the belief that we can't unite in collective struggle, and that we're locked in cutthroat competition with other workers, comes from people devaluing themselves and giving objects a life of their own.

This doesn't mean ideology is a lie. There's some truth to seeing society as objects moving around the market: it's the view of the owner of capital, who buys and sells labor power and commodities. This is sometimes called bourgeois ideology: all theories that describe the division of labor using neutral concepts like supply and demand, rather than exploitation, adopt the bourgeois point of view.

Bourgeois ideology comes from the rise of capitalism. The emerging European capitalist class had to destroy or coopt feudal monarchies, while unifying different places and classes into national markets. The universal right to speak, associate and trade destroyed the hereditary right to power and property. As the bourgeoisie created capitalism, it created a new working class. The capacity of society to create wealth increased like never before, but the bourgeoisie still had to keep it in private hands. The universal discourse of rights and freedoms was limited to a formal political process: workers weren't free to take over the social wealth they'd created.

To maintain this system, bourgeois ideology had to make its own rule seem natural and inevitable. Economic individualism, the universal competition for profit read back into human nature, suited that purpose. Capitalism isn't the first system to steal from its producers. But what distinguishes it from earlier forms of class rule is its hidden nature. In feudalism, it was very clear who grew the crops and who took them afterwards. In capitalism, we wouldn't exist without society supporting and shaping us, but society itself looks like a loose collection of individuals. "And," as Margaret Thatcher said, "You know, there is no such thing as society."

Money takes on a life of its own; objects, or the lack of them, determine the social status and psyche of their owners. The division of labor gets reduced to a series of specialized disciplines: law, political science, psychology and other fields capture vital insights about human society, but the more they accept the tenets of bourgeois ideology like property and individualism, the more false they become.

The bourgeoisie can't understand the capitalist system as a whole, since its social role depends on capitalists competing individually with each other as commodity owners. Marxist theories of ideology see workers, who have nothing to sell but their labor power, as the only ones who have nothing to lose. They have no stake in capitalism, which allows them to see the contradictions of the system as a whole. As they come to understand these contradictions, workers can create political parties that represent their own class interests.

Who are the petite bourgeois?

Between workers and rulers, there's an intermediate class that produces and reproduces itself. Its members exist between capitalist and worker, distributing goods, producing commodities themselves or working as autonomous professionals. Traditionally these strata were called small, or petite bourgeois, more as an epithet than as a term of analysis. But it's a useful term to describe the roots of localism.[16]

As a class, the petite bourgeois compete for a portion of the social product against both big capital and the wage demands of workers. Its members work as either small–holding producers or professionals. Erik Olin Wright details their trajectory in the US, where 40 percent of Americans were self–employed in the late nineteenth century. This declined to 10 percent in the 1970s, before beginning to rise again as service industries and traditional manufacturing grew. The petite bourgeoisie keeps growing for complex reasons, including the growth of precarious labor, where work previously done by full–time employees is contracted out, and the rise of information technology, allowing decentralized small manufacturing. However, this doesn't mean every petite bourgeois is self–employed. This raises the thorny issue of how to define a class that, by its very nature, falls outside the fundamental binary of capital and labor. A middle layer can't just be a grab bag for everyone who either doesn't work in a factory or vacation in Monaco. A few concepts can help clarify whom, exactly, the petite bourgeoisie is.

The French sociologist Pierre Bourdieu suggested the petite bourgeois are workers who are attempting to leave the working class by their own efforts. He names a middle stratum of "junior executives and office workers" and those who come from the working class without highly skilled qualifications. Like the self–employed, their political outlook reflects an individual strategy to get ahead. These "junior executives" closely parallel both the 'creative class' of young, urban workers in the sciences, high-tech and the arts, and what Carrlson calls the Nowtopians: "educators, computer workers, performers – a range of 'middle class' occupations.... (c)hoosing exodus from much of the work and trappings of 'middle class' success." These aren't the old petite bourgeois of small shopkeepers: the new professionals are either self-employed or engage in highly individualized labor.

Bourdieu's conducted intensive empirical research on this layer, which means he could have been too specific. The shopkeepers and executives of 1980s France may not exist in twenty first century North America. For instance, he describes the individual who *"makes himself small to become bourgeois,"* denying immediate pleasures in order to save and invest, in the best tradition of the parsimonious capitalist. But this doesn't describe all petite bourgeois. Estill's web designers and yoga instructors sound quite generous, and sometimes they produce commodities outside of a large division of labor. However, scientists, engineers and counselors aren't all petty-commodity producers. They're often not self-employed and have surplus value extracted from their labor power like all workers.

These concerns raise a more fundamental problem: Marx is often accused of writing about a society of capitalists in top hats who command male workers in overalls. Can a theory of labor exploitation even exist with today's self-employed, professionals and innumerable other job categories, where who works independently and who sells her labor power isn't always clear?

Wright suggests class location is contradictory, with two different kinds of middle class people. First are the self-employed and the "'old' middle class," who "are neither exploiters nor exploited." The second category includes people who do both. Professionals or the "'new' middle class" may not have capital themselves, but they exploit the skills of other workers beneath them. This puts them in a contradictory relation to both capital and labor, where they take on aspects of both. This doesn't solve the problem entirely: there are still those middle class professionals who have a material interest in exploiting those beneath them, even though they're exploited themselves. But it suggests that while the term 'middle class', encompassing everything from income to cultural traditions, is too broad to be useful, the label petite bourgeoisie captures that stratum's contradictory relationship to the division of labor.

The politics of the petite bourgeoisie

The vast range of jobs in a middle stratum is bound together by one thing: a lack of independence. Big capital sets the conditions for getting credit and achieving SNALT. The petit bourgeois lack the clout of either labor or capital, whether they're small–scale merchants or highly paid professionals. This means they have a collective identity, but one based on a shared experience of a *lack* of collectivity. Like the bourgeoisie, the petite bourgeoisie is structurally prevented from seeing its relationship to the division of labor. It operates around the edges of the capital–labor relation: unlike the working class, it helps circulate small amounts of capital through its small businesses, or it helps coordinate production as technical staff. It encounters commodities as part of their distribution, not production. Because of this, the petite bourgeoisie can see the symptoms of capitalist growth but not the causes. Therefore it tries to alleviate those symptoms, not overcome capitalism.

It's important to remember that this analysis applies to a social relation, not a job category. Marx wrote that petite bourgeois politicians don't have to be petite bourgeois themselves: "According to their education and their individual position they may be as far apart as heaven and earth. What makes them representatives of the petite bourgeoisie is the fact that in their minds they do not get beyond the limits which the latter do not get beyond in life." The class's "education and their individual position" can vary: capital's boundaries, and the hard choices of those facing those boundaries individually, are set in stone.

Underlying the petite bourgeoisie's myriad of cultures and occupations is a desire to *avoid* class conflict. Class members feel that what's good for them, being able to save and advance through their own merits, can help everyone. This makes sense, given the petite bourgeois confront the class struggle as outsiders, without the weapons of capital or collective organization. The small business owner can get along if big capital stops undercutting her prices and unions stop driving up her taxes: free the market of these imperfections and everything will work just fine. Caught between the struggle of capital and labor to appropriate the social surplus, the petite bourgeoisie isn't powerful enough to abolish either. Instead it tries to drive that conflict away and create social peace. Therborn suggests it's not a coincidence that, outside of social crisis, the petite bourgeoisie demands "cheap credit, antimonopoly legislation or agriculture and other subsidies," all central themes for localism. The petite bourgeoisie suffers under the power of big capital and its bureaucracy and legal apparatus, so it promotes the values of restraint, limitation and autonomy, its own political goals.

Habitus

There's no single ideology for the different layers of the petite bourgeoisie. However, localism is a petite bourgeoisie ideology because it projects its particular class interests, the desire to remain small and avoid conflict, onto the capitalist economy as a whole. This assumes cultural, not just economic forms.

Habitus was a concept Bourdieu invented to describe how ideology works. The simplest definition is the taste of class: what members of a particular class do to define themselves. This means everything from going to university, to their favorite music, to what kind of beer or scotch they drink. But habitus also separates classes from *each other*. For a world divided into social classes, habitus helps "organizes the perception of the social world." Lifestyles come from habitus, and while they appear as a free choice for individuals, in fact they're products of a complex set of meanings that produce ideology. These meanings come from the power and privileges of their makers. Property ownership gets transformed into a series of symbols that grant cultural power to the owner. This is a description of power structures, not a way to blame people for holding certain ideas, and certainly not the "petite bourgeois ideology" so loathed by the New Left. It's simply that individuals who move up, apparently by their own efforts, come to believe that those who behave and consume appropriately can do the same.

Those who control capital don't have to rise because they're already at the top, while those without capital are stuck selling their labor power to survive. Bourdieu ascribes multiple, shifting ideas to the petit bourgeois precisely because they're constantly moving between the two poles, rising up or falling down the social hierarchy and using habitus to mark their progress. Habitus is about the consumption of goods and images, and this departs from Marxism's focus on who controls production. But for a class that distributes capital, rather than making or owning it, this is appropriate: for the petite bourgeoisie, control over consumption substitutes for real social power.

Stuck between capital and labor, the petite bourgeoisie's class power is limited by the power of other classes. This forces its members to personalize all decisions about how to advance. There are no family networks to inherit capital through or collective communities to depend on. They face daily "ethical, aesthetic or political dilemmas" that determine their well–being and future prospects, making everyday life into a series of strategic decisions. Members of the petite bourgeoisie assume that the sum of their voluntary choices creates social change. Put together, these choices equal a lifestyle, which both legitimizes those who practice it and models that behavior for others. Its 'lifestylism' makes the petite bourgeoisie unique: it is the only class to demonstrate these values not through propaganda and overt control (which it will never have) or collective resistance; instead it seeks "its occupational and personal salvation in the imposition of new doctrines of ethical salvation." Thus, Bourdieu writes, "the new petite bourgeoisie is predisposed to play a vanguard role in the struggles over everything concerned with the art of living, *in particular, domestic life and consumption.*" (Emphasis added)

When localism substitutes ethical consumption for politics, this isn't an error: it's an ideological reflection of how the petite bourgeois structure their lives. The new professional classes don't plan or control production; instead they owe everything to getting the right qualifications, through the partial meritocracy of education. Their younger, more progressive members enjoy all activities that reward self–improvement, time and public demonstrations of goodwill such as charity work. This makes sense, because they are assigned to "tasks requiring precision, rigour, seriousness, in short, goodwill and devotion." Without capital, their ethical system thrives on thrift and self–discipline, what Bourdieu calls an "economizing mentality," as they restrict their income to rise up through the ranks. Self–denial creates a part of localist ideology as, for example, when Schumacher calls for "being much less greedy and envious ourselves; perhaps by resisting the temptations of letting our luxuries become needs; and perhaps by even scrutinizing our needs to see if they cannot be simplified and reduced."

This doesn't mean all petite bourgeois are self–denying; they are often liberal and big–hearted. However, what marks localism as petite bourgeois is its individualism. Without the collectivity of community ties, or the deep social power of possessing capital, the petite bourgeois is forced to survive as an individual, as Bourdieu argues: "He is convinced that he owes his position solely to his own merit, and that for his salvation he only has himself to rely on." That tension may not form the basis of the gentle, small–scale trading community that localism idealizes. But it's an undercurrent, providing urgency to the message.

By substituting lifestyle for politics, the petite bourgeoisie is drawn towards personal, rather than collective action. Bourdieu links its "prudent reformism in politics" to a morality based in self–discipline, subordinating immediate desires to get ahead. This doesn't mean the entire petite bourgeoisie is localist. However, petite bourgeois solutions to social and ecological crisis are features of localist ideology. Both pro– and anti–market localists draw on the values that help the petite bourgeoisie accumulate: individualized moral judgment, voluntary simplicity, community and ethical lifestyles.

Morality
When Proudhon confronted the contradiction between his ideals of free and fair exchange and the reality of monopoly capitalism, he praised what was good in capitalism and abandoned the rest. Schumacher repeated this 125 years later, opposing capitalism because of a moral judgment: "now that we have become very successful, the problem of spiritual and moral truth moves into the central position." For lack of wisdom, as the basis for morality, humanity creates "a monster economy, which destroys the world" through "greed and envy" that drives war and competition. The misuse of land derives from a lack of a "firm basis of belief in any meta–economic values," leading instead to economics as the sole judge of worth. A true recognition of our humbleness is required: "Man is small, and, therefore, small is beautiful. To go for giantism is to go for self–destruction." Capitalism should value human need instead of mass production. He can't explain how capital will create better uses; he just hopes people will come to share his moral economics. The disease of capitalism isn't exploitation but "the neglect, indeed the rejection, of wisdom... by allowing cleverness to displace wisdom, no amount of clever research is likely to produce a

cure." Wisdom "can be *found* only inside oneself," before which "one has first to liberate oneself from such masters as greed and envy."

There's nothing wrong with Schumacher's moral compass: his distress is a human reaction to the tremendous waste and suffering capitalist economies create. Marx devoted large parts of *Capital Volume One* to the horrors of child labor in factories. However, Marx saw capitalism as a system whose all–consuming need to generate value creates exploitation, growth and crisis. Without that understanding, localism mistakes capitalism's consequences for its causes and hope wisdom and morality will correct it. That judgment becomes intensely personal and gets turned back on humanity as a whole. Kingsolver castigates the human species for being "good at making our dreams manifest and we do, historically speaking, get what we wish for. What are the just deserts for a species too selfish or preoccupied to hope for rain when the land outside is dying?" As individuals, we assume responsibility for the entire system: "we automatically become accomplices of the devastation that is wrought on the earth by the spread of unsustainable agricultural methods." So many of us have failed that the culture is at fault: "Global–scale alteration from pollution... happened after unrestrained growth, irrespon- sible management, and a cultural refusal to assign any moral value to excessive consumption." Our lack of goodness allowed this state of affairs to happen in the first place, as Schumacher writes: "If we permit (land mismanagement by agribusiness), this is not due to poverty, as if we could not afford to stop them; it is due to the fact that, as a society, we have no firm basis of belief in any meta–economic values."

Even anti–market localists follow this logic, substituting the spread of bad ideas for historical investigation. Carrlson is clear that "the dominant capitalist system" leads nations and corpora- tions to get their way at any cost, "up to and including mass murder." However, the problem is still in our hearts: "we also carry and reproduce dominant assumptions and norms about property and individual freedom that are powerful impediments to inventing a new life based on a common wealth." The new life may be collective but the obstacles to achieving it are individual. Once "dominant assumptions and norms" are identified as a stumbling bloc, it hardly matters whether the cause is socialism or Buddhism. We have failed in our heads before we even act upon the world.

We must be very bad to have allowed industrialism to rule for over a century. Schumacher dismisses structural reasons: "A great shout of triumph goes up whenever anybody has found some further evidence... of unfreedom, some further indication that people cannot help being what they are and doing what they are doing, no matter how inhuman their actions might be. The denial of freedom, of course, is a denial of responsibility." This responsibility extends from our sense of right and wrong to our intellectual understanding of the world, and even to what we put in our mouths.

Freedom of choice, and the need to shoulder personal responsibility for our crimes, resonates with some familiar religious tropes, leading Schumacher to call his system Buddhist economics. According to Kingsolver, the "conspicuous consumption of limited resources has yet to be accepted widely as a spiritual error, or even bad manners." We have transgressed, not only against the planet but also against our very souls. The judgment of Buddha or Christ awaits our poor consumption habits: "California vegetables are not the serpent, it's all of us who open our veins to the flow of gas–fueled foods, becoming yawning addicts... We seem to be built with a faulty gauge for moderation." Having yielded to "the serpent," the appropriate action is to repent; yet "(h)ow is it possible to inspire an appropriately repentant stance toward a planet that is really, really upset... The cure involves reaching down into ourselves and pulling out a new kind of person" with the values of thrift and self–restraint. This is a direct, if unconscious echo of the habitus Bourdieu sees in the petite bourgeois, who deny their needs to get ahead. But here that self–denial does far more than help individuals: it has the power to redefine humanity.

Voluntary simplicity

According to localist ideology, our greed caused the ecological crisis. To solve it, Schumacher says we must live differently, "scrutinizing our needs to see if they cannot be simplified and reduced." There's no distinction between rich and poor; indeed, Schumacher speaks against "universal prosperity" because it doesn't provide security. The rich "have never felt secure against the poor" and the poor have nothing to lose from committing crimes. Wealth mobilizes science, technology and rationality to eliminate ethics. Note that Schumacher isn't condemning the misery and struggle of poverty but the lack of social peace that conflict brings.

The answer is self–restraint, which creates quality interactions. As McKibben describes a localist society, you "may not have quite as many small appliances, because they may cost a few dollars more, but you'll be happier." The lack of possessions dovetails with a nostalgia for the past when "people felt a little constrained about showing off wealth." The past was a realm of balance and harmony: "we may be able to re–create at least some of the institutions that marked, say, Adam Smith's Britain, and hence create some of that moderating sense of responsibility." Apparently debtors' prisons, the poor house and church–based welfare created responsibility; no doubt the poor felt very responsible when they had to bother the rich for handouts. McKibben even lauds the Great Depression for how it boosted social solidarity, but "we don't want another Depression even if it would have an excellent effect on morale." Petite bourgeois ideology becomes an iron fist in a velvet glove: a gentle reminder to the rich to tone down their conspicuous consumption, with a wistful look back to when the poor knew their place.

Voluntarism

Capitalism creates its own contradictions, and by joining struggles of the oppressed and exploited, anti–capitalists try to both reveal those contradictions and win a hearing for their analysis. As Marx famously alliterated, "Here is the rose, dance here!" We begin with society as it is, not as we'd like it to be. Voluntarism means substituting one's own personal projects and priorities for building social movements, rather than trying to understand and change conditions as they exist right now.

The petite bourgeoisie lives in a world where personal sacrifice is supposed to yield rewards. Localist schemes live what 'ought to be' in the present, and this act comes to stand in for political strategy. What Carrlson calls the "new social forma-tions" are composed of people with the privilege to stand apart and create their own schemes: those who have distanced themselves, voluntarily or otherwise, from their jobs and relieved "themselves of the pressure to conform to a hostile ideological culture." He names "bicycling activists, free software developers, biofuel advocates, etc. (who) are either themselves well–educated, or are the children of the professional stratum. But 'professionalism' has lost its hold… (and) people are walking away."

These well–educated professionals share the same individu-alist strivings of their class, except in reverse. Carrlson quotes a Portland, OR activist who claims, "Most, but not all (bicycle activists) have an upper middle class background. They all have a comfortable enough life that they can spend time doing this. They can play." Sandwiched between capital and labor, yet outside the labor process itself, the petite bourgeoisie is free to romanticize work, turning it from a compulsion into fun. Speaking of small–scale farming, Roberts lauds "a way of life that connected with great forces in the universe, not simply a way of making a living." As if to compensate, the localists pride themselves on how hard and messy their work is, which is only an option if your regular job isn't dirty or dangerous. Kingsolver says gardening requires a similar sacrifice, taking "hours bent to our crops as if enslaved," yet proving "addicting" in the end. Carrlson criticizes this kind of moralism, explaining that promoting sacrifice and suffering allows free workers to feel "morally superior" to those unwilling to do the same. Yet this is no different than the morality of self–sacrifice that afflicts the petite bourgeoisie as a whole.

Community

We've seen how localist reform schemes run up against the limits of capitalism: its incessant devouring of workers and smaller competitors in a bid for temporary stability. It wouldn't be capitalism without a drive to expand, centralize and control. Localists have trouble acknowledging this, and it's easy to see why. For the pro–market localists, people can be empowered through ethical market choices; admitting the market *destroys* individuals would be contradictory. Anti–market localists are clearer on how capitalism works but believe we can step outside the market to defeat it. Both are wrestling with powerlessness: faced with the unpalatable conclusion that small alternatives won't outcompete or destroy capitalism, localists cling to a fierce faith in communities to band together and do it yourself.

Marx's description of alienation anticipated the localist yearning for community, freed from the uniform mediocrity of anonymous, corporate–controlled spaces. However, the petite bourgeoisie's way of life precludes a community, since members of the class rely mainly on themselves for economic progress and emotional support. Community members are either fellow petite bourgeois competitors or customers demanding lower prices. Perhaps this why so many localists have such a strong nostalgia for community as an ideal place where business happens and values take shape. This desire for a mythical home life pervades localist literature: McKibben says, "think of yourself as a member of a community, and you'll get a better deal. You'll build a world with some hope of ecological stability, and where the chances increase that you'll be happy." Farmers' markets aren't just a place to shop, but a place to socialize: since "consumers have *ten times as many conversations* at farmers' markets as they do at supermarkets... You go from being a mere consumer to being a *participant*." Activist opposition to "commerce" is inspired by the "drive for community and innovation." The wealthy will even take responsibility for the poor again, once they have to live next to them. Local economies ease alienation: "local economies equal community, which in turn equals a better shot at deep satisfaction."

Why do localists want their shopping trips to include personal conversations? Alternately, you could appreciate the anonymity and speed of supermarket transactions if you have other ways to socialize. But it makes sense that the petite bourgeois, trying desperately to succeed in the marketplace or gain control on their own merits, would feel lonely. They try to re-forge the social connections lost in the marketplace in the same individual way they advance. The work of the petite-bourgeoisie is, as Bourdieu says, "the competition of antagonistic pretensions": set against workers, big capitalists and each other, the petite bourgeoisie's first concern is the profit margin: how close it is and who's pushing them towards it. Their weekends, if they're lucky enough to get them, are spent buying vintage furniture, hiking boots and lawn spotlights. Consumption is where they compete to achieve the symbols of habitus. The desire for friendly consumption is as close as the petite bourgeois get to stepping outside their daily antagonisms; yet it's not really an escape. Doing your part for the planet where friendly farmers are happy to sell you $6 eggplants can become the latest marker of habitus in a never-ending battle for status and mobility.

Just like ideology is a single class's way of life generalized to all of society, community for the petite bourgeois becomes community for them alone. Schumacher conflates industrialism and cities, blaming them for "the growth of a city proletariat without nourishment for either body or soul." Estill's ideal small town is full of entrepreneurs pursuing "a meaningful living for one." Wendell Berry goes further, criticizing corporations, governments and schools for concealing a "private aim (which) has been to reduce radically the number of people who, by the measure of our historical ideals, might be thought successful: the self–employed, the owners of small businesses or small usable properties, those who work at home." This persecution of petty capitalists sets local community advocates against "Communists and capitalists (who) are alike in their contempt for country people, country life, and country places. They have exploited the countryside with equal greed and disregard." The local community are "small farmers, ranchers, and market gardeners; worried consumers; owners and employees of small businesses; self–employed people; religious people; and conservationists."

The inference is clear: the working class isn't part of the community. The images are of the town square, the main street where everyone knows your name, the butcher, baker and small shopkeeper. These evoke market towns where residents distributed commodities made elsewhere. In contrast, industrial towns were often centers of intense class struggle between owners and workers. Not coincidentally, industrial towns created close community networks forged in that struggle. These close–knit communities of workers also demonstrated all the values of collective self–sacrifice, yet localists never mention them, preferring fuzzy invocations of consumerist fantasy.

The problem lies in how malleable the term community is, including capital, the state and workers, groups whose interests are fundamentally at odds. By suggesting workers are at most another group making demands on the state, the designation of community hides power relations. It replaces class with innumerable differences of income, culture and other sociological categories, bounded by geography rather than a common exploitation. This blurring of conflict is fundamental to localism. Pluralism and participatory democracy, pillars of liberal ideology, rest on groups remaining small, since becoming too big can drown other voices out. But this is the point of class struggle: capitalism itself has arrayed vast forces against each other on an ever–shifting terrain, and in fighting to make themselves heard, workers' groups must become big to oppose capital as loudly as possible. By invoking community, localism attempts the political equivalent of Proudhon's fair markets for small artisans, imposing a false social peace by eliminating the working class rhetorically.

Lifestyle

Bourdieu thought the petite bourgeoisie expressed its habitus through proper "domestic life and consumption." Localism provides many ways to live ethically. Kingsolver idealizes "farm nostalgia… a secret longing for some connection a to a life where a rooster crows in the yard." She even writes a chapter on the restrained, eco–connected lives of the Amish. Both she and Petrini think we should go "back to the land." But Petrini goes further, turning an ideal rural life into ideology and stamping his own class outlook on everyone else. As a gastronomist, he thinks everyone should become gastronomists. Since we've lost sight of what makes good food, Petrini's consumer is a hero: "there is only one figure who can unite and concern everyone: the *new gastronome*." Foodies form communities, which link up and form a world network embracing different cultures. Alienation begins to ease: "when we start to lose the feeling of being alone… and we are able to work in the name of our community of destiny, no business, no change, no machine will be able to stop our quest for happiness."

More far-sighted localists realize that their lifestyle doesn't accomplish these lofty goals. Smith and MacKinnon state that "I am not deluded enough to feel that I'm *making a difference* or *being the change I want to see in the world.*" Despite "travel(ing) these ethical pathways" for twenty years the environment continues to deteriorate, "and my *being* has done little to *change* the world." Yet they have no other alternative, instead repeating their main premise: "The problem everywhere nowadays turns on how we shall decide to live." Faced with the failure of ethical lifestyle choices, the answer is more of the same choices.

The localist lifestyle is another way to ease the loneliness of individual class striving, rather than a way to stop capitalist degradation. This explains why each localist promotes the specific benefits of her lifestyle: after all, that lifestyle assuaged her particular experience of alienation. Permaculture technologies, DIY bicycle repairs and biofuels production, open-source software writers and the Burning Man festival in the Nevada desert: these are all wonderful things to do, but what ties pro- and anti-market localists together is a desire to escape alienation *within* capitalism because they can't see a way out.

At its most radical, lifestylism results in a highly personal anti-capitalism, as eclectic as the lifestyles themselves are varied. This can be given a political gloss. Carrlson draws on Marxist theorist Antonio Gramsci to argue that cultural politics can create a new anti-capitalism. Subcultures alone aren't enough, but alternative lifestyles "are essential precursors to a broader political movement, though none of them is a guarantee that such a movement will happen." This is the crux of every lifestyle argument: culture will one day erupt into political change. However, culture is not lifestyle. Gramsci, a leader of Communist Party of Italy, defined culture as a broad network of social institutions, such as education, technology and science that reflect and shape class society. He saw culture strategically, calling on the Party to create institutions that could counter the influence of the state, capital, fascists and the church. Culture wasn't a series of individual choices on how to live, but a realm of collective struggle at the heart of capitalist institutions.

An inward–looking, personalized version of culture fits well with the petite bourgeois mindset. Writing on lifestyle anarchism, Bookchin suggests the petite bourgeois's individualism leads them to see lifestyle as a way to freedom, substituting the personal satisfactions of the ego "for social institutions, political organizations, and radical programs, still less a public sphere." Instead of thinking strategically about the contradictions of people's lives, and where the basis for "social action" might be, the petite bourgeoisie follows a set of instructions on how to behave, steeped in moralism and based on "individual autonomy rather than social freedom." How one lives becomes an act of propaganda.

When the gap between individual and social freedom yawns, anti–market localism retreats into longing. Carrlson ends his discussion of lifestyles by hoping for "a harmonious and peaceful transition to a sensible, humane, and comfortable life for everyone," where we can "consciously redirect our collaborative energies to a world of our own design." However, a "politically savvy Nowtopia has yet to appear." It's not a coincidence that, at the very moment it finally asks *why* the world hasn't changed, localism falls silent. Its honorable socialist sentiments dissipate in the billions of individual lifestyles that would need to change, by its own slow, adding–up process, in order to overturn entrenched capitalist power.

By refusing to think collectively, Bookchin argues that lifestylism looks like neoclassical economics. The individual ego becomes what needs to be freed, and this "turns out to be identical to the 'sovereign individual' of laissez–faire individualism," achieving the "'selfhood' of petty–bourgeois enterprise." In fact, the very promotion of lifestyle occurs when the petite bourgeoisie is most integrated into the capitalist economy, which relies on the "myth of individual freedom" to conceal exploitation. The petite bourgeoisie is *"entirely captive to the subterranean market forces that occupy all the allegedly 'free' terrains of modern social life,* from food cooperatives to rural communes." The idea that freedom could be built in the margins of capitalism comes from the petite bourgeois desire to impose social harmony on the massive, contradictory forces of capital and labor.

Utopianism

Faced with its heavenly ecstasies being drowned in the nexus of cold cash payment, the petite bourgeoisie flees into fantasy. The power of its moral vision does nothing to the power of capital or labor; instead, its must content itself with ideas alone. The frustrated petite bourgeoisie finds relief through utopianism: the attempt to create ideal societies where the contradictions of capitalism don't exist.

Marx and Engels knew and appreciated early nineteenth century utopian thought, which came from a ruthless condemnation of existing capitalism. Engels praised the "three great Utopians" Saint–Simon, Fourier and Owen. Their schemes for social change may have included turning the oceans into lemonade, but they also wanted social, not just political equality. As Engels wrote, "It was not simply class privileges that were to be abolished, but class distinctions themselves."

Marx contrasted utopianism and social science: the latter investigated existing social conditions; the former drew its plans from the imagination of its theorists. The utopians set their plans against the world at large and then condemned that world for not sharing them. Since their criticisms were abstract, their solutions were too. They thought society was irreparably damaged and proposed a "perfect system of social order" imposed through propaganda and model experiments. In contrast, Marx studied political issues drawn from the struggles of people themselves:

"We do not confront the world as doctrinaires with a new principle and call on them to kneel before it in admiration: we develop new principles for the world out of the principles of the world itself." Those who "confront the world as doctrinaires" create the terrain of struggle in their own heads, not the world. Without an analysis of the forces shaping the world, utopians simply contrasted the dark present with the rosy future, with their own plans as the bridge. They couldn't trace present reality from historical development, making plans that existed out of time, as Draper says "in the form of pious wishes of which one couldn't say why they had to be fulfilled right now and not a thousand years earlier or later."

Engels didn't blame the utopians for not understanding how capitalism worked: at the time they were writing, capitalist social relations hadn't developed to the point where deep-seated antagonisms were visible. The same can't be said of present-day utopians, who set their plans for nations of small businesses or cities of community gardens against the real development of capitalism.

This doesn't mean utopias are false: as a form of ideology, they come from how classes relate to the division of labor. For example, Proudhon didn't just mischaracterize capitalism as a system of small-scale trading. His solutions, a national credit society and labor-money, anticipated the new society without dealing with the contradictions of the old: namely, the global drive to achieve SNALT that undercut direct labor schemes. But this appealed to the petite bourgeoisie, which saw its hard work undone by large factories able to produce more cheaply. As Marx wrote, the "petty bourgeois... views the production of commodities as the absolute summit of human freedom and individual independence." The class wanted to receive all the value it put into its goods, an impossible task since capitalist production constantly tries to *remove* value from commodities and lower their price. With no way of understanding large-scale production, let alone ending it, the petite bourgeoisie had to create models at the margins of society. It designed blueprints for community life, run by the petite bourgeois themselves. Some acknowledge their debt to this tradition: Hahnel, although a critic of localism, nonetheless believes "the past thirty years has weakened the case for scientific socialism even further, and greatly strengthened the case for utopian socialism, and it is time for anticapitalists to adjust our thinking accordingly."

Unfortunately, there's no material basis for that thinking. Localism's schemes try to remove participants from the capitalist division of labor. The philanthropists may be in charge, as in Estill's intentional community owned and operated by small–holders. Or localists may hope that small, voluntary projects agglomerate. Shuman recognizes that ethical business raises costs and leaves local businesses open to takeover. But strong local laws and "public education and peer pressure" of "enlightened share-holders" will protect local businesses. These shareholders won't be driven by profit but instead the desire to "presumably know, appreciate, and even honor many of their neighbors" and "make more community–friendly (investment) choices."

Here we see utopian localism in action. Large businesses must achieve lowest cost production and will move to do so. Small businesses do not, or at least they aren't supposed to, but even they can't be trusted. Political action will force them into enlight-enment. Where does that political action come from? The respon-sible shareholder. Where does the shareholder gain responsi-bility? Education. Centralization and rent will disappear when enlightened capitalists see how much damage they cause. Localism's values of community and voluntary simplicity are an attempt to impose a moral order on capitalist exploitation, while standing outside of it. In its espousal of small projects harkening back to a pre–capitalist economy, localism is a modern form of utopia.

Catastrophism and crisis

The problem with utopianism isn't just that imagining a future society avoids a political discussion on how to achieve it. It has a real, psychological impact on the utopians themselves: when the gap between real and imagined grows too large, they start to fantasize about the end of the world.

Model–building, in of itself, doesn't define a utopia; rather, utopias embody the desires of a frustrated class. The logic of creating alternative values with no means to implement them comes from a society undergoing change from above. Utopians criticize dominant trends from a position of powerlessness, lapsing into what Raymond Williams calls "sentimental 'desire'," helping them to reconcile with their own alienation. He thought that post–1968 utopias were defined by their hopelessness: emerging from the defeats of left–wing movements, they questioned the very possibility of changing the world. Rather than transforming a wealthy society into an equitable one, they rejected all wealth as corrupt. These kinds of futures transform an imaginary world, not this one. They don't speak to the vast majority who don't have their basic needs met: they appeal only to those experiencing a crisis of their own power.[17] Localism represents the striving for self–power of a class seeking social peace and not finding it. After 30 years of neoliberalism, when capitalist power has grown immensely and seen off all challenges, localism has become tinged with despair. Even imaginary worlds are far–off hopes: some immense catastrophe is far more likely, such as peak oil or climate change, which will end a system out of control.

There's a contradiction here: a sense of immanent catastrophe doesn't sit well alongside individual solutions to social crisis. After all, if small lifestyle and consumption changes truly can change society, then there's no reason to panic. It is only when the scale of the crisis becomes clear that the petite bourgeoisie's mild reformism collapses into something darker. Having never considered capitalism as a system of exploitation of the majority, and suspicious of mass movements by its nature, the petite bourgeoisie abandons hope and awaits social breakdown.

McKibben summarizes the last 100 years: "the old accommodations with state capitalism and social democracy that twentieth century working class politics settled for, are closed. Global climate change, war, crashing biodiversity, waste and industrial pollution, mass starvation, and epidemic disease are just the top of a long list of pressing reasons to radically change how we live on earth." The earth's peril signals that politics is over. Kingsolver suggests we "all may have some hungry months ahead of us, even hungry years, when a warmed–up globe changes the rules of a game we smugly thought we'd already aced." Climate change will destroy "basic industries like agribusiness, oil, chemicals, automobiles, asphalt (and many more), (which) will probably contract suddenly, often into total collapse." Speaking of the world's poor, Schumacher enthuses that "they are survival artists and it is quite certain that if there should be a real resources crisis, or a real ecological crisis, in this world, these people will survive. Whether you and I will survive, is much more doubtful." Even Carrlson's optimism is tempered with disaster: the "foundations (of a new world)... are solidifying... at least as fast as the planet is descending into chaos."

Of course, the earth *is* in peril. There is plenty of evidence that capitalism is overrunning the ecosystem's ability to regenerate. Marxists have said for over a century that capitalism is such a fundamental contradiction to human life that it will destroy us all. Rosa Luxemburg, a leader of the German Social Democratic Party (SPD), argued in 1915, "Today, we face the choice exactly as Friedrich Engels foresaw it a generation ago: either the triumph of imperialism and the collapse of all civilization as in ancient Rome, depopulation, desolation, degeneration – a great cemetery. Or the victory of socialism."

Luxemburg opposed both a blind faith in market progress,

and a belief that the absolute, physical limits to growth will bring down the system. She rooted crisis in social dynamics: when producers create commodities that can't be sold, the system swings between boom and bust, moving "in the direction of its own ruin." She assumed capitalists need new markets to absorb excess exchange–values and didn't consider that capital can recover through new forms of internal exploitation or destroying existing, less efficient facilities. But her insights, and those of the many Marxist theorists who came after her, showed how capitalism survives its crises by offloading them onto workers and the environment.

From this perspective, the localists are in good company. With continual crisis, it makes sense to fight for complete change: if "the socialist transformation is... the consequence of the internal contradictions of the capitalist order – then with this order will develop its contradictions, resulting inevitably, at some point, in its collapse." Substitute 'bioregion' or 'network of small communities' for "socialist," and the argument still holds: capitalism creates the seeds of its own destruction, and radicals should organize to replace it.

It appears strange, then, that the only localist to engage with crisis theory opposes it. Hahnel says governments can spend to prop up demand, and thus "the idea that capitalism contains internal contradictions that act as seeds for its own destruction is simply wrong and needs to be discarded once and for all." He may be an avowed anti–capitalist, yet Hahnel echoes the ideology he wants to dispute, because neoclassical economics depends on not seeing crises or inherent contradictions either. Without them, the system may be unfair, but it's fundamentally stable: all anti–capitalists can do is propose new ways of living and hope enough people listen. The economists agree and don't waste time building alternatives.

Luxemburg wryly suggests, "the people who abandoned Marx's theory of crises only because no crisis occurred within a certain space of time merely confused the essence of the theory with an inessential particularity." Taken charitably, this suggests political economy is just confusing; however, more insidiously, acknowledging the roots of crisis means acknowledging the power big business has to shape the terrain on which small firms, ethical or otherwise, have to operate. Hahnel is committed to building alternatives now, so he may have made "inessential particularity" central to his analysis. This is a shame, because if capitalism does offload its crises, it creates the possibility for change. What matters is how people respond.

Unfortunately, most localists don't even get this far. Without the tools for social investigation, they throw up their hands and feel helpless. This is a natural response to disaster, tempered by a liberal optimism that makes the coming apocalypse a vindication of localist schemes. "In so many ways, disaster makes us take stock," Kingsolver writes. "For me it had inspired powerful cravings about living within our means." For localism, catastrophe will rebalance the books. In a model concerned with size, the problem is excess. Estill glows with anticipation for the coming holocaust: "Resource depletion, societal collapse, and impending doom may just be the best thing that ever happened to 'community'." Carrlson sees disaster providing the push needed to create a new, local, ecological society.

The recent Peak Oil thesis has provided catastrophism with new life. McKibben argues that high oil prices will end large–scale agriculture. Peak oil is useful for pointing out the absolute limits of a carbon–based economy. However, this shifts the focus of production to its technical limitations, precisely what capital strives to overcome. As 2010's BP oil spill in the Gulf of Mexico shows, higher prices will push capital to exploit resources further afield, regardless of the horrific consequences. If the question is posed as a problem of who uses what, without addressing who has the power to dictate those uses, then consumers become the problem. Localist catastrophism, like localist social change, is individual: humans have consumed the finite amount of resources available and can't live rationally. This fundamentally conservative view of human nature has deep roots.

Malthusianism

Thomas Malthus was a nineteenth century parson with one purpose: to remove the natural rights of poor people to survival. He said the poor were inherently greedy and lazy. They couldn't control their impulses to breed, so the population would quickly outstrip the supply of food, compete for scarce resources and starve. As industry grew, it would remove workers from agriculture, decreasing food production just when it was needed the most. Social welfare made matters worse, creating inefficiency in the natural supply and demand of the means to live. If the poor couldn't find food, it was best that they die; to this end, Malthus called for the end of the poor relief law and to deny social assistance to children born a year afterwards. If poverty was natural, then changing it was worse than useless: reforms would just generate thieves, eager to steal from the worthy rich.

Malthus eventually backed off from his call for a social cull: he felt that with moral restraint, the poor could become wealthy. But that morality only appeared in the market: competing for their own survival would increase the poor's energy and virtue. Having gone through this cleansing, the rich were morally fitter than the poor. Cutting social welfare not only saved money, it was good for the poor themselves, who would be forced to restrain themselves and get a job. Malthus managed to turn poverty from a social ill into the moral responsibility of poor individuals.

The idea that humans are by nature greedy is a tenet of Malthusianism, neoclassical economics... and localism. Human appetite is voracious: Kingsolver observes, it "is both extraordinary and unsympathetic in our culture to refrain from having everything one can afford." Schumacher follows his training as an economist of scarcity: "as physical resources are everywhere limited, people satisfying their needs by means of a modest use of resources are obviously less likely to be at each other's throats than people depending upon a high rate of use." Natural laws dictate social use. McKibben goes further, reducing our social nature to a machine: "viewed in one way, modern Western human beings are flesh–colored devices for combusting coal and gas and oil." Animals or machines, we are subhuman. Deep ecology echoes these ideas, with its stringent criticism of industrial size and goal of reducing the number of humans. Compare these sentiments to Malthus on the poor's insatiable appetites: "human institutions… are mere feathers that float on the surface, in comparison with those deeper seated causes of impurity that corrupt the springs and render turbid the whole stream of human life." There is no hope for rationally organizing a society of people intent on consuming everything in sight.

The point of this crude socio–biology is to make capitalist social relations natural, hiding how poor people might have come to be to poor in the first place. Bookchin argues that, for deep ecologists, human history is just an expanding machine and capitalist laws get wiped away by "an all–devouring civilization." As with Malthus, petite bourgeois ideology makes moral judgments of individual behavior. It's not just that we're wasteful, but that our wastefulness is a *moral* failing. As Schumacher describes it, "is the sin of greed that has delivered us over into the power of the machine." He can't understand how richer societies can't quell "the frenzy of economism," and why their rulers don't create more humane forms of work. The problem must be in our hearts. This describes the effect of capitalist expansion but not its motive. The goal shifts from understanding how to resist capitalist exploitation to "moving towards saintliness." Generosity and selflessness may allow good people to sleep at night, but in a system that's fundamentally *amoral*, values can't explain how it works. Lacking this explanation, localism projects its confusion outwards, drawing some dubious philosophical parallels.

Not all localist politics end in catastrophism or Malthusianism. An aspiring member of the professional classes would have difficulty rising up if she was fixated on failure and social breakdown. Rather, these are possible dystopias ingrained within localism, the logical binary of its utopianism. Their purpose isn't to make localists abandon homemade jam, credit cooperatives or farmers' markets; rather, catastrophe and greed provide an undercurrent of fear to *motivate* these changes, showing what will happen if localism doesn't work. They correspond neatly to the petite bourgeoisie stuck as an intermediate stratum, the internal tension of self–denial that Bourdieu says can appear as "asceticism and Malthusianism." Localism shows how powerless people trapped between capital and labor feel.

Localist moralism: the locavore

When localists aren't listened to, consumers change from the solution to the problem. Kingsolver is scathing about the food decisions of poor people: "we complain about the high price of organic meats and vegetables that might send back more than three nickels per buck to the farmers." Meanwhile, "if many of us would view this style of eating (local food) as deprivation, that's only because we've grown accustomed to the botanically outrageous condition of having everything, always." She recognizes that consumption rises to deal with stress of working lives, but "much of it simply buys the services that make it possible for us to work those long hours." The capitalist imperative to increase productivity turns into its opposite, a personal choice of workers themselves.

Since consumer preference determines everything, the localists judge other people's non–local lifestyle by their own aesthetic preferences. Schumacher disapproves of "complicated tailoring" and suggests clothing should be "the skillful draping of uncut material." Our possessions shouldn't be "anything ugly, shabby or mean." Kingsolver calls buying portable music players, high–speed Internet service, large vehicles and name–brand clothing "categorically unnecessary purchases." Since the radio is enough for her, it's enough for everyone. All of consumer culture is a form of "teenage boy culture" geared to flashy, pointless things. Continuing the theme of adolescence, Carrlson quotes an expert: "'our whole society is like a teenager who wants to have it all, have it now, without consequences," promoting "a shallow hedonism" to encourage mass consumerism. We are less than adults, thanks to our consumption choices. Localism pursues a familiar vision of ideology here, where everyone else is brainwashed except for the wise.

A concrete example of localist moralism is food politics. The petite bourgeoisie's judgments on food stem directly from its habitus. Kingsolver is adamant that everyone can choose good food if they make cooking a recreational activity. For those of us with free time, a "quality diet is not an elitist option for the do–it–yourselfer" since, in most of the world, the wealthy eat pre–prepared food while the rural poor cook for themselves. For the poor, "home–cooked, whole–ingredient cuisine *will* save money. It will also help trim off and keep off extra pounds."

There's a long history of social reformers trying to shape working class behavior. In *The Housing Question*, Engels criticized how reformers reduced social ills to personal morality. He didn't minimize the horrible standards of living that working class people endured. Rather, he blamed their bad habits on that environment: "under existing circumstances drunkenness among the workers is an inevitable product of their living conditions, just as inevitable as typhus, crime, vermin, the bailiff and other social ills." Moral exhortation and "building model institutions" encouraged artificial class harmony through which workers would accept their lot rather than agitate for change. Conditions didn't change for most English workers until social reform legislation was passed but, in the meantime, education and moral improvement allowed the bourgeoisie not to blame itself.

In 1930s England, there was a public debate on how the unemployed could change their diets to cope with having less money. Orwell wrote:

Would it not be better if (the poor) spent more money on wholesome things like oranges and wholemeal bread or if they even... saved on fuel and ate their carrots raw? Yes, it would, but the point is that no ordinary human being is ever going to do such a thing. The ordinary human being would sooner starve than live on brown bread and raw carrots. And the peculiar evil is this, that the less money you have, the less inclined you feel to spend it on wholesome food.

The problem wasn't ignorance but the psychology of class:

When you are unemployed, which is to say when you are underfed, harassed, bored, and miserable, you don't *want* to eat dull wholesome food. You want something a little bit 'tasty'. There is always some cheaply pleasant thing to tempt you.... *That* is how your mind works when you are at the P.A.C. (social assistance) level. White bread–and–marg and sugared tea don't nourish you to any extent, but they are *nicer* (at least most people think so) than brown bread–and–dripping and cold water. Unemployment is an endless misery that has got to be constantly palliated.

Orwell knew this was an "appalling diet" and that the results were "a physical degeneracy." He decried those who "pour muck like tinned milk down their throats and (do) not even know that it is inferior to the product of the cow," and he didn't absolve "the modern industrial technique (of food production) which provides you with cheap substitutes for everything." This had been ably exposed by Upton Sinclair in *The Jungle* 30 years earlier, just as it's exposed in today's criticisms of fast food. But arguments about nutrition and ecology miss the point: the need for "cheaply pleasant things" suggests social reality is more complex.

Bourdieu examined how food choices are a consequence and not a determinant of class. It's true that the richer you are, the smaller the proportion of your income goes to food and your consumption of cheap, fatty foods declines. It's not only about having enough money, because people with similar incomes consume differently. It is, however, about the class background of the consumer. Those "who are the product of material conditions of existence defined by distance from necessity" are able to enjoy "the tastes of luxury (or freedom)." Those who've never worried about surviving can relax and explore new kinds of consumption. In contrast, those whose lives are governed by need consume the "taste of necessity": what fulfills that need in the short term. "Thus it is possible to deduce popular tastes for the foods that are simultaneously most 'filling' and most economical from the necessity of reproducing labor power at the lowest cost which is forced on the proletariat as its very definition." If you don't have to sell your labor power, one of the freedoms you gain is the taste for good food.

Ignorance of this relationship confounds the locavores. Those pursuing the taste of luxury are so used to "absolute freedom of choice" that they can't even understand "the taste of necessity," whose consumers "have a taste for what they are anyway condemned to." The compulsion of wage–labor makes taste "a forced choice, produced by conditions of existence which rule out all alternatives as mere daydreams and leave no choice but the taste for the necessary." Failure to grasp this forced choice allows localists to pose a moral one, as Kingsolver argues: "For a dedicated non–cook, the first step is likely the hardest:

convincing oneself it's worth the trouble in terms of health and household economy, let alone saving the junked–up world." It's true this is the hardest choice, but only because the taste for the necessary doesn't come from a rural idyll where the "greatest rewards of living in an old farmhouse are the stories and the gardens." For lack of an old farmhouse, Petrini argues, "Should anyone be tempted to ignore the complexity of the world and consume their food irresponsibly and unfairly, indifferent to social justice, I say that the fair has become indispensible." Those who don't share the expectations of class mobility are irresponsible and unfair.

Commodity fetishism, the basis for habitus and its choices, gets erased in favor of a nebulous and ever–present culture, morality and laziness. Food localism becomes the latest sign of "class racism" against the 'sheeple' who are too brainwashed to know what's good for them. Decades before localism rose to prominence, Bourdieu wrote that the working classes who buy pre–packaged food at grocery chains

> ...are the people 'who don't know how to live', who sacrifice most to material foods, and to the heaviest, grossest and most fattening of them, bread, potatoes, fats, and the most vulgar... (and who) fling themselves into the prefabricated leisure activities designed for them by the engineers of cultural mass production; those who by all these uninspired 'choices' confirm class racism... in its conviction that they only get what they deserve.

There is no difference between criticizing an unhealthy diet and criticizing one that doesn't come from the proper, local place. In fact, local food is even further from the taste of necessity, since it's a moral obligation to taste and the environment, not just to one's own health.

The localists acknowledge this strategy's limits without an

explanation. A commentator on Schumacher recalls that when *Small is Beautiful* "was first published, many thought that change would come through insight, logic, compassion, and reason. Increasingly, it seems that change will come about after we have exhausted every other theory of greed and gain...That the world should become so immune to its own losses seemed inconceivable 25 years ago." Greed and gain rule the world despite the good intentions of the localists. Carrlson admits:

> The over–arching assumption of early adherents (of permaculture) seems to have been a belief that by doing good work well, the rest of the society would 'get it' and come along. After a quarter century the movement has spread... But the dominant society hasn't lost its grip on the underlying priorities, values, and decisions that shape global capitalism. If anything, the rape of the planet is proceeding at a faster pace than ever.

This heartfelt passage captures the hopelessness of those opposing global capital with worthy, moral projects. Who wouldn't despair at watching profit destroy the planet, while feeling that the last 25 years of resistance haven't amounted to much? Bourdieu suggests that the petite bourgeois get disillusioned as "they grow older and as the future which made sense of their sacrifice turns sour." There's no impugning the motives of the petite bourgeoisie: their personal sacrifice, creating schemes that are supposed to grow, comes at great emotional cost. The next step of looking for someone to blame seems only natural, and what better target is there than the poor and the working class, who for some strange reason continue to shop at Wal–Mart and eat at McDonalds? The judgment of individual consumer choices forms a complex of taste and morality, allowing localists to blame people in general for ecological destruction. This reaction is understandable from a personal, moral perspective.

But it's also a political gift to the Right, who can pose as defenders of individual freedom against holier–than–thou liberal elites.

Petite Bourgeois hegemony

Engels felt that due to the development of large–scale industry and the working class, the utopians were archaic and would disappear. Yet if petite bourgeois ideas are so narrow and contradictory, how have they become popular?

Gramsci's analysis of hegemony helps explain why. Hegemony is ideology that works through culture, politics and economics to make workers agree to being governed, without physical force. Gramsci suggests that the petite bourgeoisie has a unique role to play in propagating ideology by *becoming* intellectuals.

When a ruling order disintegrates, different forces jockey for power and classes campaign to prepare society for their ideas, shaping "political analysis and popular experience" into a unifying force. This is what Gramsci calls a war of position. A petite bourgeois war of position is impossible: the class has too many internal contradictions. However, petite bourgeois intellectuals can still assert those *inconsistent* ideologies, reflecting how the class is drawn in different directions.[18] Today neoliberalism has silenced the organic intellectuals of the working class, while neoliberalism's crisis has opened space outside the dominant capitalist triumphalism. In this space, localism is the petite bourgeoisie's war of position. Having dismissed working class struggle and class society itself, individualism is the unifying spool around which the disparate threads of petite bourgeoisie ideology wind.

Not all localisms are petite bourgeois; not every member of the petite bourgeoisie is a localist. Localism isn't dominant today because of its social power. Instead, the decline of working class movements has created an ideological space for localism.

Localists themselves may be radical anti–capitalists, but their theory is a form of what Bourdieu calls "enlightened conservatism." Isolated consumers have to confront capitalism "untrammelled by the constraints and brakes imposed by collective memories and expectations." They don't have to plan anything other than their own accumulation strategies and have abandoned any collective defence against the market. In the place of historical traditions of class struggle, the petite bourgeoisie's voluntarist ethos allows localism to promote small lifestyle choices and a proper moral outlook. Community and voluntary simplicity provide a neat fit with localism's criticism of size, and an implicit judgment of working class behaviors and appetites. Darker streaks of catastrophism and Malthusianism infuse it with terror when necessary.

Since localism comes from the life practices of an intermediate class, it doesn't consider the alternative that Marx did: collective struggle to replace capitalism.

Chapter Five

Building Socialism from Local Spaces

The economics of localism ignore capitalist laws of motion, and the ideology of localism reflects the hopes and fears of the petite bourgeoisie. What about localism's politics? In a neoliberal age, localism helps fill the gaps that market deregulation creates. Even radical localist theories like postcapitalism, Solidarity Economics (SE) and Participatory Economics can end up bolstering neoliberal ideas when they fail to examine how capitalism works. But if small–scale alternatives can't change the world, this doesn't mean local spaces are irrelevant. When local activism opposes capital rather than avoiding it, it creates the potential to build a better world.

Some localists recognize that capital has a lot of power. For example, economists Anne Bellows and Michael Hamm recognize it's impossible to establish local, democratic control over the food supply without "economic democracy" to counter "the principle of accumulation of wealth" and "challenge(s) systemic inequities." But they offer no way to challenge those inequities beyond "conscious public framing" i.e. telling people about them. Similarly, Daly and Farley run into trouble when dealing with property rights. They point out that raw materials are owned privately, while disposal sites like the atmosphere and oceans are public. It's better to cut waste at the source rather than try to clean up afterwards, but this would mean interfering directly with private property. "Should we advocate revolution then?" they ask but don't answer. Instead, they call for property rights that "can belong to individuals, communities, the state, the global community, or no one." Owning something is a way to exclude others from using it, and just listing bigger and bigger owners doesn't get around this, while the last category ends property altogether. Daly and Farley hope for "suitable policies (that aren't)… limited only to those that require private property rights." That's unlikely to impress current owners, who may want to keep their properties and have the right to acquire new ones.

These economists approach the limits of capitalist property and then back away. The question they want to ask is: how can we oppose capitalist power? To answer that, we first have to look at how the capitalist state wields power, and how it's used localism for its own ends.

Neocommunitarianism

Every society needs to coordinate production and distribution, but the scale of a developed capitalist economy puts that task beyond the ability of any single firm. The capitalist class, which needs the proper conditions to sustain profitability, must cede direct authority to a state. The state manages crises, creates infrastructure and provides subsidies to industry. However, this kind of economic intervention can only go so far: too much might eliminate the private sector or lead people to question why we need it. As more and more workers are drawn into production, the process of establishing and maintaining control gets more important. This is another major role of the state: to protect private property and maintain class power. It deals with threats from the dominated classes through laws, social welfare and occasionally the police and military.

After World War II, states in the Global North were broadly Keynesian, based on a compromise between capital and labor. Capital introduced new production techniques without fear of socialist take–over, and in return for labor's peace, the state created near–universal social welfare. As part of these provisions, central government took responsibility for local problems. But in the 1970s, falling productivity and class struggle created the twin dangers of stagnation and inflation for global ruling classes.

Competition between capitalist firms intensified to the point that profits fell and growth halted. Yet capital still had to make a profit, and to reduce its taxes it forced apart the Keynesian compromise. It lowered the social wage, the combined welfare benefits that people got from the state. The Keynesian bureaucracy may have provided social welfare, but it was also a way to control poor people. Right–wing ideologues seized on this, pointing out how alienating and unfeeling these institutions were and suggesting this was a direct result of their massive size. The problems Keynesianism set out to solve became its fault: now poverty was an outcome of state intervention.

This is better known as neoliberalism. Against dehumanizing institutions, the neoliberals claimed to take things back to genuine democracy by letting the market solve all our problems locally.[19] Neoliberalism made production cheaper by allowing firms to move where wages were lower. But it also made *reproduction* cheaper for the state. By cutting back on social programs, neoliberalism shifted the costs of workers' lives onto workers themselves, making them pay more for childcare, education and old age expenses. Or it eliminated those services entirely and made workers provide them for free.

Neoliberalism pushed production across national boundaries; increasingly, cities produced for the world, not for the locality around them. But this expansion came at a cost: to create larger production processes, capital needed to plan even more aspects of production, from raw material sourcing to educating workers. Keynesianism couldn't create this urban infrastructure effectively and neoliberalism still struggles with it. But by enforcing global market rules on local spaces, neoliberalism redefined social problems. Where big government couldn't help, local people could help themselves in the social economy: community–level initiatives outside the state and big business that focused on building micro–enterprise, often cooperative and non–profit. Localism equates small with progressive; so did neoliberalism.

Bob Jessop calls this process neocommunitarianism, where states harness the grassroots social economy for economic development. Keynesian states also funded grassroots activists, but neoliberal states are more careful: they promote local initiatives with only small amounts of funding. That money goes to encourage the social economy to retrain workers and regenerate cities. Cities end up competing against each other to create a pro–market environment and attract wary investment dollars; if they don't, capital can always go elsewhere. Within strict market limits, cities bring in private, voluntary groups to do what national governments used to, replacing publicly provided services and building training networks.

This doesn't mean social economy activists want more market rule, but building lasting non–market initiatives are very difficult. Local development needs wealth, institutions and people with the means and connections to make local projects work. Where job prospects, social mobility and government support are weak, the social economy stagnates. Poor, disconnected people don't get careers just because they have a project to participate in. Lasting local development requires complex, deep economic and social links in manufacturing, state regulation, wages and so on. That requires money, something neoliberalism makes sure that local social economy programs don't have much of.

Capital gets to be universal, demanding subsidies, expensive regeneration projects and flexible labor markets. Local communities remain responsible for social and ecological problems. These problems mean that slowly expanding local social enterprises is what Hahnel calls "a utopian pipe dream." Decentralization becomes part of neoliberalism's deep, structural changes, unleashing market forces that will fix all social ills. This is why governments are warming to "localism, localism, localism": not as an alternative to neoliberalism, but as a way to *implement* it.

Postcapitalist localism

While neoliberalism was using the local, social economy for its own purposes, a radical theory appeared to help. Postcapitalism started by criticizing a key premise of classical Marxism: that anti–capitalism can only happen at the point of production. If workers stop work, they stop producing surplus value and the system grinds to a halt. However, as Marxist–feminists have pointed out, this ignores reproduction. Workers don't disappear after work: they need to eat, sleep and raise the next generation of workers. This has traditionally been seen (or rather, *not* seen) as women's work. The home and community are also workplaces for nannies and other 'caring professions': value gets created outside the formal, public realm, in private spaces. The line between production and reproduction gets blurry. The home and community, and not just the workplace, are sites for anti–capitalist struggle.

This is a vital insight for describing how the working class actually works, so it's worth examining how some localists have used it. Economists J.K. Gibson–Graham, writing as one author, suggest that traditional economic analyses, both neoclassical and Marxist, focus solely on production.[20] But where production is global and abstract, the local is diverse, the place people actually create their lives. Since all production and reproduction happens somewhere, global and local aren't fixed categories. They get continually redefined and recreated, and how we see them depends on what direction we look from. Look at these categories differently and we can redefine them, freeing ourselves from the tyranny of one discourse or one activity.

For Gibson–Graham, looking at the structural limits of political economy gets in the way of "enacting postcapitalist futures." Instead, we have to see capitalism "as uneven, fragile, and less extensive than imagined" in order to "imagine, act, and claim new spaces of intervention." The "less singular and solid analysis of power" of poststructuralism, and its political alternative of postcapitalism, gives us power to act. Systems of power with internal logics of their own become bad things, not because capital exploits labor, but because learning about them makes us feel hopeless. For example, they cite a feminist who says the feminist movement isn't anti–capitalist enough. This makes her an "unwitting coconspirator" with globalization who suffers from "paranoia" because she conflates feminism with the overwhelming logic of capital. John Holloway, a Marxist, suggests, "radical theory tends to focus on oppression and the struggle against oppression, rather than on the fragility of that oppression." By seeing capitalism as fragile, we can create politics with "a new kind of dispersed collective action that (does) not depend upon the organized revolutionary agendas of more established radical politics."

Postcapitalism means, first of all, talking about capitalism differently. Gibson–Graham say the problem with the Left is that it's "capitalocentric... in which already existing economic alternatives are seen as no different from capitalism, supporting or shoring up capitalism, or so opposed as to be utopian and thus unrealizable." To oppose this we need a new form of "language politics... a new, richer language of the diverse (not exclusively capitalist) economy." Without being so fixated on capitalism, we can find places "where alternative cooperative and intentional economic activities coexist with multinational capitalism." The local is both where we are and where we should be.

Gibson–Graham go in search of "noncapitalist imaginaries." They send researchers to a deindustrialized region of Australia to visit the unemployed and break their binary mindset. The researchers can't say they work for a university, which would provoke anger at state institutions. Gibson–Graham call this "the narrative of 'our' victimization at the hands of 'them'." Instead, they tell one "political" man, bitter at the industrial policies that threw him out of work, to give free car maintenance classes. No longer trapped, "he has moved toward pleasure and happiness associated with a different economic way to be... position(ing) him as skillful and giving, and endowed with an economic identity within a community economy." The unemployed can become a "resource," just as powerful as capital, because they spend their benefits locally. Once the workers have abandoned "the State, Capitalism, and Power" as categories, they can form a "micropolitical opportunity... that call(s) the naturalness or suffi-ciency of one's own identity into question." That new identity is based on simple acts of generosity: "a meal that was consumed by its producers (created) unwitting involvement in the practice of collectivity." Together the unemployed workers form "the hopeful subject – a left subject on the horizon of social possi-bility."

It's true: studying how capitalism works can make you depressed. A world where talking about things differently changes them would be a great place to live. But, unfortunately, capitalism works beyond the level of our individual perceptions. It has to: as Marx identified even before he studied political economy, capitalism is defined by alienation, the separation of our innate selves from production and from each other. In fact, Gibson–Graham are engaging in idealist philosophy, which says that the motive forces of history and society come from the ideas in our heads. In a way this is liberating: we can make society different with the power of our good intentions. Marxism, on the other hand, is a materialist philosophy, which says our social relationships come from the way we organize our material existence. Capital does indeed have limits beyond our heads, but since a global working class creates the world through its activity, that activity can be studied and organized according to our collective needs. This creates a flowering of historical, political and strategic questions, an empowering possibility that Gibson–Graham cut off. Instead, acknowledging the power of capital equals being powerless.

Gibson–Graham argue that local politics "will go nowhere without subjects who can experience themselves as free from capitalist globalization." But this form of subjectivity is precisely what capitalism makes impossible. Capital itself is capitalo-centric, acting well beyond the local. The American Federal Reserve and a community garden federation don't have equal power; volunteer farmers can't shut down a state that subsidizes agribusiness. Gibson–Graham claim "local initiatives can be broadcast to the world and adopted in multiple places across space... And global processes always involve localization—the arrival of the McDonald's outlet on the next block, the local link–up to cable TV, the building of a factory on customary owned land." But McDonald's outlets, cable TV and factories don't just arrive in one locality rather than another: capital's drive to accumulate embeds them in a constellation of social relations in different spaces. The very localization of those global processes causes social crises, as capitalism's contradictory, seesawing development invests in a region and leaves when production prices lower elsewhere. This is what victimized the hapless "political" man. Perhaps, with enough time, energy and institutional coordination, he and his neighbors could support each other by giving away their skills. But in a capitalist economy with complex, socially defined and most importantly profit–oriented needs, there'd be little guarantee of success.

There's also a deeper political issue, whether the angry man could scrape a living outside the market or not. Why should capital be allowed to land where it pleases, exploit labor, strip resources and leave? Postcapitalism removes reproduction from capital's balance sheet, abandoning the legions of unemployed desperate for work on the worst possible terms. Gibson–Graham ask, "If we viewed the economic landscape as imperfectly colonized, homogenized, systematized, might we not find openings for projects of noncapitalist invention?" Of course:

capital is quite happy to let workers survive without paying for it, and one of the pillars of neoliberalism is that workers need to stop blaming the system and start looking after themselves. But perhaps the unemployed and deindustrialized are right to ask capital to pay for the privilege of using and abandoning localities.

Finally, postcapitalist localism says that politics and economics are male domains and focusing on them leaves out women. This is true: women have been, and continue to be, marginalized in ways too numerous to list here. However, precisely because the political economy of capitalism structures women's lives in brutal ways, it's too important to ignore. A truly feminist theory does more than show women coping with oppression: it understands how women come together to resist it. That resistance begins at the local, but it doesn't end there.

Rosa Luxemburg castigates those would who adopt "the morality of the bourgeoisie... the reconciliation with the existing order and the transfer of hope to the beyond of an ethical ideal–world." Postcapitalism's ideal world helps reconcile workers with the existing one. The political alternatives based on it do too.

Solidarity Economics

SE recognizes that neoliberalism destroys local economies by encouraging low wages, factory closings and environmental damage. Workers often survive outside the market by relying on each other in "self–organized relationships of care, cooperation, and community." For SE, neoliberalism can be transformed by deepening those relationships. Ethan Miller is clear that ethical businesses and cooperatives can't "out–compete" capitalist firms. But "this does not mean we shouldn't play the capitalist game as it now stands." Two things are needed: "a *transformative social movement* capable of changing the culture and economy," and worker co–ops that can operate "successfully in a capitalist market" to support it.

This is a powerful argument: social movements need all the help they can get, and worker coops can be important sources of financial and institutional support. However, to "feed the 'bottom–line' of the financial ledger *and* advance the cause of social and economic justice" isn't entirely straightforward. Here, an acknowledged position of weakness is turned into a strength: SE claims that enterprises with "barely a prayer" of competing can still operate "successfully in a capitalist market" and "achieve victories that no solely oppositional 'resistance movement' can ever achieve."

What are these "victories" based on? Miller advocates an ecosystem vision of the economy in which natural resources, production, exchange and consumption are part of "a cyclical whole." Unlike Marx's vision of capital circulation, this cycle is biological, not social. Categories like "creation", exchange and investment are torn free of power or exploitation. Investment is no longer a battle to realize above–average profits, with overproduction and crises as a result: it's simply "the recycling of surplus." Profit doesn't exist: as Miller states, production is simply "human transformation of resources into goods and services." A holistic economy is a balanced economy where inputs equal outputs.

This is exactly like the neoclassical model: capital gets interest, labor gets wages and there's nothing left over. Yet SE also acknowledges a surplus that, according to Miller's own ecological model, shouldn't exist. In capitalism a surplus can only mean exploitation, the appropriation of surplus value from the working class. This is precisely why neoclassical economics had to do away with surplus and create the concept of equilibrium in the first place. Miller brings it back, with no explanation of its source or how it fits into a steady–state ecological model.

The focus on holism does away with classes and class struggle. Socialist politics is seen as "simply... advocating for alternative institutions of production." Despite criticizing socialists who reduce everything to economics, SE begins to sound 'economistic' on its own: "(a)ppropriate to this holistic picture, movements working for a just and democratic economy must generate interventions – and link these interventions together – at every point of the economic cycle." Since the economy is no longer a site of power, strategic questions about how, where and why to intervene disappear. SE turns away from capital to find "existing economic practices – often invisible or marginal to the dominant lens – that foster cooperation, dignity, equity, self–determination, and democracy." In an epistemo-logical leap that's never explained, these values arise naturally from "organizing across the entire economic ecosystem and building a broader social movement." This means creating "reliable... solidarity markets" for goods and services produced by worker cooperatives, which move from "entering markets" to constructing them.

How can tiny organizations, democratically–run or not, construct markets already constructed and occupied by capital, particularly when Miller recognizes that capitalism can co–opt movements for mutual aid? The answer is, once again, small: capital overlooks the local. In an admission that somehow has no bearing on the entire theory, Miller allows, "it is not easy work, of course—*especially considering the demands placed on worker–owners by a cut–throat competitive market*—but it is the work that we as cooperators must embrace if we choose to believe that another economy, and another world, is possible." (Emphasis added) Cornering a capitalist marketplace relies on Gibson–Graham's voluntarist tautology: it works because "we choose to believe" that it works. The real world imposes far more limits, as Carrlson recognizes: "(e)fforts to break away, to create islands of utopia (be it socialism in one state, or co–ops, collec-tives, and other smaller–scale social alternatives) have always flourished on the margins of capitalist society, but (have) never...

been able to supplant market society's daily life." This is clearest when SE proposes actual intervention schemes.

Lisa Stolarski, an SE advocate, agrees that it doesn't really matter if unions and cooperatives aren't "in a position to take on the market domination of Capital." Instead, SE provides "a weed and seed project designed to uproot the unjust power dynamics of Capitalism and replace it, enterprise by enterprise, with creatively organized cooperatives that serve the needs of people." The ecological metaphor obscures capital's scale: now, "enterprise by enterprise", cooperatives will eat into the capitalist market. Local innovations will form "always–broader collaborative networks and solidarity chains," becoming "structurally effective for social change." Unions will use their dues–base to fund co–ops, while co–ops will use union funds and skilled union labor to make better products and "maximize competitive advantage... efficiency and increase revenue in the competitive market." In turn, the unions can use co–ops to help organize industries.

Neoclassicals say capital and labor are factors of production: they provide the same utility and can be substituted for each other. It follows that workers can become capitalists by amassing and investing enough money. This describes how SE works in the social economy: worker–run firms will prosper because there aren't any private shareholders demanding dividends and lowest–cost production. Therefore, workers' wages can rise while the firm saves money. Cooperatives can grow by reducing employment, creating a labor shortage and raising wages for workers inside and outside the cooperative. Even without outside credit, a union–cooperative alliance can support workers during bargaining and buy firms that capitalists themselves have written off. According to SE, this will gradually restrict whole sectors of private industry.

However, this is a fantasy. In a market controlled by oligopolies, even workers at social enterprises must maximize their efficiency and revenue. Shareholders and creditors aren't simply leeches: they provide the capital necessary to keep pace with technological change and, more importantly, to out–invest competitors. The capitalist firm has a much bigger pool of educated workers to choose from, and it can lay off workers when it doesn't sell its products. Social enterprise has none of these advantages.

Of course, the law of value doesn't coerce all workers the same way: in cooperatives, workers own their factories and shops and decide democratically how production is organized. Marx saw them as transitional between private and shared ownership, modeling how an economy could be run democratically. However, in capitalism cooperatives also make workers discipline themselves to meet the lowest–possible market prices. Marx didn't speculate on whether they could compete successfully with capitalist production. More soberly, Soviet economist Evgeni Preobrazhensky said that because of the overarching power of the global market, cooperatives don't create new forms of production and exchange.[21] Instead, they're simply "small islands not of social but of collective–group ownership of the instruments of production," tolerated "in the sea of capitalist relations *only in so far as* they are so subordinated." Swimming in a sea isn't the same as draining it: cooperatives only survive by meeting globally–set production prices and can, at most, redistribute a small portion of profit. For example, Spain's Mondragon cooperative has an annual turnover of $1 billion US and controls the nation's largest grocery chain, but it still has to adapt its business practices to EU free–market directives. They may provide the power of a good example, but cooperatives don't eliminate the need to achieve SNALT.

The slow adding–up of social business also appears in Shuman's *Small–Mart Revolution*, which scales up his small–business economy to conquer the world. Small businesses provide training and technical support to communities in the

Global South to help them transform agriculture away from export to staple crops. Networks of independent businesses, distribution and micro–finance create firms strong enough to "buy out chain stores and reorganize them into global networks of locally owned businesses." Exactly like SE, small business expands and, due to the superior use–values of its grassroots networking, overcomes economies of scale. Credit is neutral, not a tool to reinforce capital's rule. There's no struggle to control the surplus. Shuman cites Switzerland as a country "where many small businesses control the nation's economic power" and which encourages "community self–reliance." SE wants to eventually replace the capitalist market; Shuman wants to use it. Both pro– and anti–market localism express the petite bourgeois view of capitalism: small–scale entrepreneurs and social enterprise can expand indefinitely, everywhere.

Ironically, both models rest on a neoliberal assumption: that the creation of niche markets can protect producers from pressures to achieve SNALT. It's true that plenty of companies make goods more costly than the average: these goods provide a key part of habitus, distinguishing upper from lower class. But high consumer prices simply reflect higher–cost materials and production, limiting sales to a smaller, wealthier customer base. Would this be an acceptable goal for SE or Small–Marts? Meanwhile, the well–paid cooperative workers or entrepreneurs would be under constant threat as capitalist competitors developed new machinery and management to lower production costs.

Stolarski's plan makes unions responsible for restructuring the labor market while Shuman reproduces this fallacy on a grander scale. Cooperatives and small enterprise are supposed to accomplish what decades of union struggle could not: making "the wage market... too expensive" and forcing capitalists out. Spare a thought for the poor capitalist who may, under the compulsion of exceeding average profit rates, be forced to undercut small, social enterprise.

How does SE deal with SNALT? Gibson–Graham's ethical force reappears: Stolarski suggests "forming the hopeful subject" as a response. The working class has to stop worrying so much about the power of capital, overcoming "barriers... within us, in our own thinking and attitudes." These include misunderstanding the advantages of credit and capital to workers, and the "(m)isunderstanding of all profit–making as being Capitalistic in nature." Once we abandon our capitalocentric attitudes, we learn that credit is a neutral tool for workers rather than a tool for centralization. But exploitation is more than a misunderstanding. By relying on idealist philosophy, SE puts profit back to its neoclassical roots: as a return on factors of production.

There's a political question at the heart of SE's confusion. Stolarski argues that trade unions and cooperatives "have lost sight of their critique of capitalism and their calls for liberation from the wage relationship." However, trade unions never wanted liberation from wages: their role is to negotiate the terms on which workers sell their labor power. That gives them a vital role in the anti–capitalist movement as an incubator of working class organization and politics. But they're not, and never were, revolutionary. Stolarski implies that *economic* organization is sufficient for revolution. As she argues, "The working class possesses everything we need to create wealth and social prosperity in our own interest." If this were true we would have socialism tomorrow. But the working class lack social and political control: this is what defines its members as working class, forced to sell their labor power to the owners of capital. By claiming liberation is within our grasp, right now, SE elides the crucial *political* transformation of workers through class struggle that makes them anti–capitalists. Without politics, the decades of attacks on the union movement and the left don't matter. We can build it now.

The tongue–tied left

SE is dedicated to "anti–racism, feminism, queer liberation, environmental justice… and other movements." It wants to abolish neoclassical economics. These are all worthy goals, so how does it end up supporting capitalist ideology?

Bourgeois social science splits economics and politics: one side belongs to business executives, the other belongs to politicians. Localism accepts this split, trying to see past capital's economic power by looking for local spaces where that power doesn't exist. However, local spaces and micro–market structures are precisely what neoliberal governments promote. Gibson–Graham positions subjects "as skillful and giving, and endowed with an economic identity within a community economy." Miller calls for "self–organized relationships of care, cooperation, and community." Neocommunitarianism promotes public–private partnerships, linking government, NGO and community groups on the basis of "solidarity." Who's co–opting whom?

There's a historical answer. After World War II, the American Left suffered a drastic decline in working class militancy, as capital accumulated, incomes rose and immigrant and working class communities fragmented. A ruling class offensive stamped out the 1960s and 1970s New Left's attempt to revitalize itself. Neoliberal ideologists lumped together social democratic parties, Stalinist regimes and radical movements alike in a bid to reassert market rule. They were successful: by defeating trade unions, cutting public services and divesting from entire regions, neoliberalism dampened activist expectations of ever successfully challenging capital.

This attack had a theoretical impact too, as localism emerged to fill the vacuum. Postmodern Marxism, the intellectual milieu that inspires SE, emerged from the decline of those social movements. Theorists rejected a structural Marxism that pushed social movements into rigid categories. Instead, the goal was to grasp local spaces concretely. But along the way, theorists stripped Marxism of its universalist qualities, rejecting, as David Camfield argues, "claims... that capital has determinate laws of motion and that social production plays a distinctively powerful role in shaping the course of the evolution of human societies... (substituting) a decentered notion of society, and the celebration of difference."[22] The local changed from a space to analyze and resist to a free space where people could make their own world. For example, Gibson–Graham claim that migrant domestic workers who invest in community development back home are "refusing to succumb to the slave or victim mentality." But the power of positive thinking doesn't change the global division of labor that forces workers to move abroad for a better wage and send remittances home. This is the danger of postcapitalism: by trying to redefine people as social actors with real power, it redefines the much greater power of capital out of existence. In doing so, it actually reproduces the determinist, structuralist accounts of capital it loathes. By refusing to fight neoliberalism, the "noncapitalist imaginary" leaves capitalist reality untouched. The most oppressed members of the working class, local communities of poor people of color, must drag themselves out of the predicament capital placed them in, by being as flexible and adaptable as possible.

If capitalism is, as Gibson–Graham suggest, "uneven, fragile, and less extensive than imagined," why do they and SE naturalize its most destructive tendencies? We have to return to the psychology of the localists for their aversion to understanding power. It's not a move towards "pleasure and happiness"; rather, it comes from a deep pessimism:

We started out, embarrassingly, with no real desire for "socialism"... Over the last hundred years, the word has been drained of utopian content and no longer serves, as it once did, to convene and catalyze the left. This makes it difficult even to speak of "the left" or to use the pronoun "we" with any confidence or commitment. As self–identified leftists at the end of the 20th century, we found ourselves tongue–tied, not knowing who or what we might speak for.

The challenge of making socialism relevant is a hard one, but in an age of international economic and ecological crisis, and the return of revolution to North Africa, it's not impossible. Yet as the postcapitalists sank into pessimism, resourceful neoliberal theorists didn't. Their offensive against the working class created defeatism, which they harnessed at the grassroots to lower their welfare costs. Thus it's a mistake to see localism as inherently oppositional. In its most diverse, celebratory and pro–community forms, official and radical localisms form a continuum, adapting non–market relationships for capital accumulation. By promoting local solutions to a global system, the centers of power remain free to impose market discipline: this, paradoxically, ensures a continuing need for localism. Localism can be a *strategy* of neoliberalism.

Does capitalism make us powerless?

If capitalist laws of motion operate beyond us, they could control us.[23] Anwar Shaikh sums up the perspective:

> To conceive of capitalism as being subject to 'laws of motion', it is said, is to treat a human social arrangement as if it were a machine or some physical process. This downplays and degrades the role of human beings in determining the course of events. People, not laws of motion, make history... (and) in any case the analysis of the causes of crises is too abstract an issue... for the practical politics of class struggle.

Holloway claims that some Communist Parties, like the Russian Bolsheviks, have used the laws of history to claim the exclusive right to dominate workers' movements. Despite some historical inaccuracies, he has a point.[24] Arguing against Rosa Luxemburg, Holloway says that analyzing objective laws inevitably overshadows "subjective action." Revolution shouldn't have to wait for a perfect future when the Party has started. Without objective laws to slow us down, we don't have to "think of the death of capitalism... in terms of a dagger–blow to the heart, but, rather, in terms of death by... a million rents, gashes, fissures, cracks... (it) is now: a cumulative process, certainly, a process of cracks spreading and joining up... already under way." When Marxists just look at the big picture, localism deserves praise for taking those fissures more seriously.

If the system is crushingly powerful, then analyzing how it works is a waste of time. Reject it entirely: look for the hopeful subject, stop being so capitalocentric, scream "No!" and scrabble at the cracks. But as Shaikh argues, choosing to ignore how capitalism works assumes that its rules are eternal. There's one other theory that accepts capitalism without question: neoclassical economics. It blames capitalism's power on unbridled human greed. Since there's not enough to satisfy our infinite desires, we have to compete. Capitalism allows our inner drives to unfold, creating equilibrium between limited supply and limitless demand. This conflict is natural: it "has no limits other than some unimaginable mutation in Human Nature or some unimaginable destruction in Physical Nature." Scarcity, greed and catastrophe may be the result, but that can't be changed. Pro–capitalists like this system, and postcapitalists reject it outright. But both take its surface appearance for fact. Rejecting capital may be inspirational, but it leaves the premises of neoclassical theory intact.

If we ignore capitalist laws of motion, it creates an overwhelming project of social change. If revolution is no longer in the future, it's right now. Disaster looms: as Holloway says, the "argument for revolution now starts from a much sharper sense of urgency. The existence of capital is an aggression... that... threatens to annihilate humanity completely.... (its) violence seems to be taking us... towards imminent catastrophe." Catastrophe doesn't just free us from being dominated by laws of motion; it makes us personally responsible for world–historical tasks. Murray agrees that we can't just assume class struggle exists. However, he warns against leaving it to our personal desires: "(w)ith so small an area submitted to the pessimism of the intellect, too large a zone is left to the optimism of the will." That shifts quickly to pessimism of the will: an existential resignation in the face of the huge problems facing anti–capitalists, which overpowers any advantages from "fragility."

Marx's critique of capitalism, on its own, doesn't lead to resistance. But understanding how social production works gives us a place to start, providing a social, historical and economic context to our ideas. Class struggle, beginning at the most local level, is the *only* force that can overturn capitalist rule, but it doesn't float in thin air.

Marxism helps understand the relation between subjective force and objective laws without collapsing one into the other. For example, when activists organize against the long hours and low wages of corporations like Wal–Mart, they're opposing capital's attempt to increase exploitation, and rightly so. But Wal–Mart is a sign that the market is working just fine: its centralization allows it to dominate supply chains and demand less government regulation, driving down prices. Refusing to shop at Wal–Mart or opposing its outlets opening can help retain the character of a neighborhood, but it doesn't change the pursuit of exploitation. It can even have unintended consequences, forcing capital to introduce new technologies and forms of organization to make savings at other points in the supply chain, or intensifying existing work and contributing to unemployment and job stress. Organizing Wal–Mart workers who make and distribute commodities into unions restricts the unrelenting drive for exploitation. It also doesn't allow capital to pose as ethical to retain its customers, like when Wal–Mart sells organic produce. In other words, strategies for extracting surplus value pose *political* alternatives that localist consumer action doesn't address.

Or take food activists, who focus on the production chain to create a sustainable food supply. Once food is seen as one commodity in the capital circuit, a whole number of other solutions appear: democratic controls over the finance and trade that agribusiness depends on; the struggles of food workers for a living wage; the fight for full employment and social welfare, making it more expensive for capital to exploit and pollute; these are all part of the movement to challenge capital. The local is no longer outside, beyond or an alternative to capitalism but a site of struggle against it. A Marxist understanding of how capital works puts class struggle at the heart of history, as people resist a system escaping their control. This is an *immanent* critique. It starts from inside capitalism, seeking to understand and exploit its contradictions.

Capitalism as contradictory

If understanding how political economy worked removed humans from the picture, this would turn capitalism into a mystical, natural law independent of human effort. Worse, it would imply that workers are completely integrated into capitalism. This might explain why the postcapitalists are so disturbed by political economy: it reflects their underlying fear that the vast majority of workers are unseeing consumer slaves. Iron laws of capitalist development only enforce that slavery. Exposing and organizing against them is useless: all you can do is get your friends together, build alternatives and wait for the entire edifice to crumble.

But the capitalist laws of motion don't trap us, because capitalism itself isn't an airtight, coherent system. Its own growth just widens the gap between use and exchange–value, between profit and realization, at ever–larger levels. It creates the social conflicts that govern capitalist development. In fact, by not understanding that contradiction, postcapitalism freezes the capitalist history of development, making it relevant across different spaces and times.

The socialist movement recognized early on that under-standing capitalism's historical development doesn't justify its degradation or close off possibilities for the future. Lenin, the revolutionary Marxist whose movement inspired millions to take up arms for socialism, hated capitalism. But he didn't condemn it outright: "there is nothing more absurd than to conclude from the contradictions of capitalism that the latter is impossible, non–progressive, and so on – to do that is to take refuge from unpleasant, but undoubted realities in the transcendental heights of romantic dreams."[25] It may seem counter–intuitive for a revolutionary Marxist, at the head of a party that struck fear into the global ruling classes, to defend capitalism. But that contra-diction disappears once we step back from the brutal conse-quences of capitalism and understand it as a historical force, developing the productive forces of society and preparing the ground for socialism. Capitalism combines vast *improvements* in technical capacity and social organization with exploitation and environmental degradation. Lenin argued that "(r)ecognition of the progressiveness of (capitalism's) role is quite compatible... with the full recognition of the negative and dark sides of capitalism... (its) profound and all–round social contradictions... which reveal the historically transient character of this economic regime."

We have to pause here, because Lenin can easily be accused of 'stageism': seeing society as a series of historical developments, each one better than the last, until the final historical battle creates socialism. If this is the case, capitalism should develop as much as possible; anti–capitalist struggle, like indigenous people opposing development, just gets in the way. For example, in some of his journalism, Marx accepted bad journalistic sources that said Indian village hierarchies were ancient and unchanging, and therefore he argued they needed outside colonial change.

There's nothing inevitable about socialism or capitalism. Capitalism removed blocks to social development by force, destroying pre–capitalist industry and creating a vast social surplus. This is what Lenin meant when he said capitalism "increases the population's need for association, for organization" along class lines. Capitalism socializes the working class, giving it the training and experience in collective work to run society itself. As Luxemburg argued, "besides the *obstacles*, capitalism also furnishes the only *possibilities* of realizing the socialist program." This is why Lenin denounced those who "exert every effort to show that an admission of the historically progressive nature of capitalism means an apology for capitalism... they are at most fault in underrating (and sometimes in even ignoring) the most profound contradictions."

Marx and his successors never made apologies for those contradictions. Despite his earlier Eurocentric writings, Marx also wrote about capitalism's colonial crimes and celebrated anti–colonial resistance in India, Ireland and the US. Any thought of a progressive historical role for capitalism ended in the trenches of World War I, as the collective slaughter made it clear that capitalists would rather send entire generations to their deaths than share wealth equitably. The twentieth and early twenty–first centuries have confirmed that capitalism will off–load crises onto millions of poor people, directly through wars or indirectly through famine and other so–called natural disasters. Earlier Marxists may have underestimated capitalism's survival instinct, but they saw that capitalism is completely amoral, and will expand regardless of the consequences. In fact, this is what motivated their hatred of capitalism: the potential for social development it creates is drowned in blood.

Combined and uneven development

In his later years, Marx saw capitalism would develop different societies unevenly, creating many possible futures. Leon Trotsky took this further through the theory of uneven and combined development. Capital exports new technologies and advanced industry into places that had none before, and poorer states don't have to go through the same slow process of development that rich ones did. For example, China's new stealth jet fighter is allegedly based on pieces of a downed American jet that Chinese technicians bought from Serbian villagers. But this doesn't mean that all states are on their way to advanced capitalism. On the contrary, the patchwork of development creates pockets of wealth amid large–scale poverty, and the resulting social tensions raise the prospects for revolutionary change. The recent upheavals in the Middle East, where the elites control vast business interests while prices for basic goods increase, suggest that uneven and combined development is alive and well. Capitalism creates vast amounts of social wealth that can't be invested for socially useful ends. It not only displaces poor people and damages the environment, but the use–values it does create aren't shared equitably.

Uneven and combined development also means that local anti–capitalist resistance has a big impact, because capital in the Global South is often owned elsewhere. That resistance takes two forms, broadly: first, local struggles to restrict capital's reach, including indigenous struggles to control land and water, or movements to protect subsistence livelihood. Those movements can improve the lives of those resisting and provide a model for bigger revolts. For example, the Bolivian water wars of 2005 led to national revolts that eventually overthrew the president. Rising food costs helped spark the 2011 uprisings across North Africa. Second, mass movements to reclaim the means of production try to wrest power away from capital, not just resist its predatory impulses. This includes trade union movements that, while non–revolutionary in nature, try to shift the balance from capital to labor, along with socialist movements that aim to do away with the balance altogether.

How could a future socialist society work?

As soon as socialist movements get discussed, the question immediately comes up, "How would socialism makes things better?" Some left–wing localisms have responded by working out how production can be coordinated democratically, an essential task in any society. Planning takes place on a vast scale in capitalism right now, within private firms. Anarchists and socialists want to make that process public and democratic. In a postcapitalist society, production that doesn't require wide–scale coordination could be conducted locally, while information technologies could coordinate planning between local, regional and national levels. Once workers establish democratic control over use–values, production for production's sake would disappear. Social need, not the need for capital to accumulate, could guide production priorities and scale. Where it makes environmental sense, people could choose machine or human labor production.

Janet Biehl and Murray Bookchin acknowledge that no single municipality can meet the complex needs of an entire economy, and there's a danger that small, isolated political spaces could be parochial: "thoroughgoing localism and decentralism, has conse-quences at least as unsavory as those raised by Statists." This means that how social planning happens is just as important as what gets planned. Participatory Economics (Parecon) supports democratic councils of workers and consumers to produce and distribute goods, organized into progressively larger federa-tions. This is based on the workers' councils that came out of revolutionary uprisings in Russia, Britain, Germany and elsewhere. For Libertarian Municipalism (LM), citizen assemblies democratically plan community priorities. Drawing on anarchist theorists Bakunin and Kropotkin, these democratic forms could create a society managed by communities themselves, not the state.

However, modeling a future society doesn't explain how to get there. Even an entire nation run according to equitable, localist principles would still have to deal with capitalist markets and states. Twentieth century revolutions proved that ruling classes will go to war, not only to hang on to their own power but to defeat socialist movements outside their borders. Albert and Hahnel advocate building movements to fight US militarism; however, since that discussion occupies three and a half pages out of over 400 in *Parecon*, it's clear that building "pockets of equitable cooperation," and not challenging capitalist state power, is their main concern.

Biehl and Bookchin also draw on the experience of twentieth century revolutionary movements to see that capital and the state can organize "broad social forces" against all alternatives. In those circumstances "the municipality is relatively powerless to challenge broad social forces – fighting in isolation, it would scarcely pose any threat at all." LM sees local spaces as sites of resistance, not just transformation. This transforms LM's own politics: no longer "strictly a localist philosophy," it advocates "some kind of transmunicipal form of organization" to resist the capitalist counter–attack.

LM shows that this kind of planning isn't exclusive to socialists. For example, anarcho–syndicalists pioneered the general strike as a form of local struggle in nineteenth century America and republican Spain. There's nothing inherent in either anarchism or socialism that leads to utopianism; the danger lies in failing to understand the limits that the drive for SNALT places on political alternatives. Those alternatives can run the gamut from communes to cooperatives: the question is not their technical limitations or possibilities, but whether they accept or challenge capitalist power.

Against prefigurative lifestyles

Hahnel argues "that creating minialternatives to capitalism before capitalism can be replaced entirely is an important part of a successful strategy to eventually replace capitalism altogether." He qualifies the statement, stating that it's not "always better to seek a solution to a problem outside the capitalist economy than... through a reform campaign." This is the crux of the issue: do postcapitalist alternatives only provide a different way of living for participants, or can they confront capitalism? The problem is that, by Hahnel's own admission, these schemes face limits from the market and only succeed by adopting its principles or finding non-market forms of support through donations and the free labor of their supporters. Relying on people with free time and money makes it very unlikely that those schemes will grow. Separated from this daily struggle and the contradictions it throws up, mini-alternatives can become abstract blueprints for a future society.

Looking for noncapitalist spaces creates a constant tension between those outside the system and those giving up and going back to capitalism. If capitalism is a system 'out there', then how radical you are depends on how strong your moral fiber is to resist it. As Gibson–Graham write, "(w)e can resist the view that co–optation automatically happens in the vicinity of power... through the vigilant ethical practice of not being co–opted." Ethical vigilance not only sounds a lot like petite bourgeois habitus, it's also hard to maintain in the face of a global system of accumulation. If we're already part of capitalism, we can fight it by exposing its contradictions. But if the task is to remain true to living the alternatives, sooner or later we'll slip up.

As democratic social movements become larger, they also become more effective at winning reforms. But reforms by themselves aren't enough: even militant working class movements like the ANC in South Africa and the Workers Party in Brazil made peace with capital once they got elected. Asking whether they 'sold out' and lost their ethical vigilance isn't the right question, because this assumes individuals, or even political leaders, have a moral power to shape capitalism. Capital has its own priorities: it will reward political leaders who maintain the conditions for accumulation, and it will undermine or abandon those who don't. Hahnel acknowledges that as long as economic power rests in the hands of the ruling class, reforms will be partial. However, he insists that "only prefigurative experiments in equitable cooperation... can begin to accomplish" creating new, equitable institutions. How?

For example, Carrlson praises DIY bike shop activists for being "resourceful, politically engaged, and passionate. They challenge the transit and energy systems shaped by capitalism but crucially, they are making connections in *practice* between race, class, gender, and urban life, city planning, technology and ecological reinhabitation." The moral fortitude, intelligence and passion of activists are beyond question; but are they actually challenging transit systems? Are capital and its political repre-sentatives moved to build greener transportation systems and urban planning when people build their own bikes? Teaching poor people to build bikes is a laudable survival strategy, but does it build a movement to challenge race, class or gender relations, even on a micro level? Yes and no. These spaces can be a place for alternative learning, creating new relationships and bringing new people into struggle. (They can also be incredibly exclusive spaces, turning away those who don't look or dress the right way.) But more importantly, as any activist knows, building minialternatives takes up tremendous amounts of time and energy. No matter how much activists building alternative spaces may hate capitalism, in practice localism shifts that energy to carving temporary spaces away from it.

Hahnel references 1970s socialists who debated how to build and maintain revolutionary spheres of influence in the transition to socialism. Based on the experience of the Zapatistas and other liberation struggles, he argues "the lesson for those of us living in 'the center' is that living experiments in equitable cooperation... begin the process of establishing new norms and expectations among broad segments of the population beyond the core of anticapitalist activists." Rather than wasting time selling socialist newspapers, he suggests radicals create LETS systems, worker ownership, cooperatives, Participatory Budgeting, consumer cooperatives and CSA. These have raised local standards of living, but in each case Hahnel stresses their limits, since they're embedded in the global economy. The answer is to take them further, and he references state–wide experiments in democratic economies in Kerala, India and in Brazil, which have achieved some important reforms against neoliberalism.

Mass parties that gain control of the state machinery are not experiments in alternative living. Electing the Communist Party of India–Marxist (CPI–M) in Kerala was not a local act (and may have involved the sale of a few newspapers). When the CPI–M tried to expropriate lands for an auto plant, the peasant revolt it provoked was local, but it was an act of mass defence and rebellion, not alternative living. These strategies have different goals, methods and results and rely on different kinds of class alliances, and equating them with localist experiments does no justice to either. Hahnel comes close to socialist politics when he calls for a new labor movement. However, he says union activists get trapped into small leftwing sects, so activists should join "equitable living communities" to find like–minded thinkers and be less tempted to betray workers' struggles. This moves beyond Petrini's gastronomists: radicals don't just have to adopt the proper lifestyle to get the right politics, they have to separate themselves from the society they want to change.

Our daily lives that postcapitalism focuses on are thoroughly compromised with the forces of capitalism. As Marx said, "Men make their own history... but under circumstances existing already, given and transmitted from the past." Every time we use a commodity, we participate in capitalist relations. The petite bourgeois obsession with individual status isn't just personally stifling; it dodges the most important *strategic* question. How can we overcome the powers that maintain exploitation?

For collective prefiguration

It's absolutely true that, as Hahnel argues, "critics of capitalism have got to think through and explain to others how we propose to do things differently and why (our desired) outcomes will be significantly better." But class struggle creates a very different kind of prefiguration from radical localism, because it forces activists to think about how power works, how people outside small radical circles relate to power, and how to build campaigns that appeal to people who, in partial, contradictory ways, are questioning capitalist rule.

Socialism involves the vast majority of people planning their collective future, going through tremendous struggle and upheaval. This is the crucible of revolution, which teaches people to cooperate in new ways. For example, in the Egyptian revolution of January 2011, demonstrators organized security, food distribution, childcare and medical care on their own. Women, who have long struggled against their second–class status in Egyptian society, were at the forefront of this movement; many reported it was the first time they had been free from harassment by men. The future visions that come out of a democratic, revolutionary process are always more creative and unpredictable than the pre–existing models.

Localist community alternatives can create a sense of togetherness, but so do organizing social movements that challenge capitalist power. And unlike localism, they don't rely on everyone leading the same kind of daily lives. Without the heavy weight of morality to uphold, activists can shift their attention to mobilizing political arguments to weaken the capitalist ideological agenda. As Orwell cautioned, anti–capitalism doesn't arrive fully formed: "no genuine working man grasps the deeper implications of Socialism… His vision of the Socialist future is a vision of present society with the worst abuses left out." But since we can guarantee that capitalism will create new abuses, these contradictions can provide the raw material for organizing. Rather than planning far–off outcomes, we can plan how to build movements that arise out of these contradictions.

When workers engage in struggle against capital, they can create amazing, creative examples of how society could work. Marx learned about direct democracy by studying the 1871 Paris Commune, when neighborhood and workplace councils sprang up to replace the deposed central government. The February 1917 revolution in Russia created the same bodies, called soviets, and Lenin saw their direct democracy as a way to create socialism. This kind of democratic, class–struggle prefiguration continues to this day. For example, in 2006 the state governor of Oaxaca, Mexico sent 1000 police to break up a teachers' sit–in demanding a minimum wage. The teachers and residents fought back, driving the police and government officials out of the city. The citizens formed the Popular Assembly of the People of Oaxaca, which they declared the new governing power in the state. It set priorities for the city and eventually created a state constitution before being brutally evicted by the governor's paramilitaries. The rebellion proved that workers don't need the capitalist state to govern themselves, but they do need to exercise popular control over the media and armed forces. Nearly 100 years after Lenin warned of "dual power", where new forms of self–government conflict with the existing state, the people of Oaxaca learned that their own, democratic institutions must expand or be pushed back.

Marx described the defeated nineteenth century proletariat

...throw(ing) itself into doctrinaire experiments, exchangé banks and workers' associations, hence into a movement in which it renounces the revolutionizing of the old world by means of the latter's own great, combined resources, and seeks, rather, to achieve its salvation behind society's back, in private fashion, within its limited conditions of existence, and hence necessarily suffers shipwreck.[26]

Postcapitalist schemes for micro–alternatives, lifestyle–based consumer activism and attempts to evade the law of value are all examples of ignoring capitalism's great, combined resources and proceeding behind society's back. But class struggle allows activists to learn first–hand about the strategies and principles necessary to build a movement. This kind of prefiguration embodies social justice, cooperation and community, all cherished localist values, plus one that's even more important: collective resistance. Rather than imagining possible futures, we can practice and learn about the political steps needed to get there.

Parecon, postcapitalism and SE differ on the details, but they all either reject collective struggle or define it as an alternative way of life. Marx criticized Proudhon for choosing good and bad sides of capitalism, as if it was possible to remain above class struggle and pick sides at will, harmonizing labor and capital while maintaining exploitation. As Luxemburg argues, "it is logical that (reformist socialism) should also 'try to thwart' capitalism in general, for it is unquestionably the chief criminal placing all these obstacles in the way of socialism." If localism truly wants to stop the alienation and ecological damage it sees, it needs to attack capitalism at its root.

Capitalism will not end by becoming top–heavy: somebody has to end it, and social movements winning reforms build people's confidence to resist. Mass movements to revolutionize society aren't common: however inspiring, it will take some time before the 2011 uprisings in the Arab world will make activists in the Global North reassess their dismissal of revolutionary politics. Hopefully, one of the outcomes of that reassessment will be to connect defensive struggles against the spread of capitalism with struggles to transform it. Radicals have to be flexible enough to see the anti–capitalist potential in all forms of resistance, and theoretically grounded enough to see that resistance, while vital, is not enough. Capitalism will develop unevenly, expand and centralize: what happens during that process is up to us.

The working class and Marxism

Marxists say the working class can change society. This isn't because workers are more ethical than anyone else, but because they create the commodity labor power, the source of surplus value. If they stop working, surplus value stops being produced. The working class still exists: people who own nothing and must sell their labor power to survive have never been more numerous. Unlike the petite bourgeoisie, workers are united as a class by the labor process itself, which denies their humanity and turns them into machine parts. However, since workers are also people, they can become conscious of that alienation and act against the system.

To counter some stereotypes, this doesn't mean waiting for white male factory workers to realize capitalism needs to be overthrown. Anti–capitalist resistance happens everywhere. Movements like the Zapatistas in Mexico, fighting for indigenous rights against land expropriation by ranchers and agribusiness, are inspiring precisely because they link everyday life to class struggle. When they win victories, they show broader society that resistance is possible. Coupling that perspective with a strategic perspective based on an understanding of the capitalist laws of motion can bring in other allies to challenge those laws.

There are two more concepts to clarify. First, class struggle may be the driving force behind capitalist development, but as we've seen, class is both a position and a relation. Class position shapes identity just like race, gender and sexuality. This is sometimes called intersectionality. None are less important than the others: they all shape, without dictating, how people with these identities understand them. Class as a relation describes the relationship between those who own, and those who are separated from, the means of production. It places those identities in the context of capital accumulation and resistance. This means class struggle can be a way to embrace, rather than erase difference.

Second, the end of Stalinism created a generation of depressed ex–Communists who equated revolution with tyranny, and it vindicated liberals who always felt that way. Rather than dismissing mass social change, as many forms of localism do, it's worth examining this historical legacy, to see how Russia, Spain, China and dozens of other revolutionary moments worked. How did they take power, and how did they restrict the rule of capital? This means rejecting both spontaneous, leaderless struggles that rise and fall without any logic, as well as the caricature of the Bolsheviks as a heroic vanguard carrying the light of socialism to the oppressed masses. Instead, we can learn from the rhythms of class struggle itself.

Rosa Luxemburg and social revolution

Prior to World War I, the German SPD was a mass workers' party with millions of members, parliamentary representatives, newspapers and schools. It was formally committed to socialism, but Luxemburg felt its bureaucrats and leaders had grown too comfortable; they were happier representing the German working class than ending its exploitation.

For Luxemburg, politics came from an understanding of capitalist economics. Eduard Bernstein, leader of the right wing of the SPD, thought capitalism could adapt to new circumstances, offset crises and progress indefinitely. Credit, the rise of management, the prosperity of the middle class and trade union victories meant workers were completely incorporated into a stable political system. Bernstein gave this a positive spin, arguing that people are comfortable rather than brainwashed. Either way, it followed that struggling for political power was useless. Instead, he argued, socialists should work to improve living standards, creating socialism through "the progressive extension of social control and the gradual application of the principle of cooperation."

Here, Bernstein substituted equal exchange and his own morality for capitalist laws of motion: "'Why represent socialism as the consequence of economic compulsion?... Why degrade man's understanding, his feeling for justice, his will?'" Luxemburg commented drily: "We thus quite happily return to the principle of justice, to the old warhorse on which the reformers of the earth have rocked for ages, for lack of surer means of historical transportation." Wanting justice didn't change capital's need to offload its crises onto the working class. This doomed the SPD's strategy of gradual change to failure, with dire political consequences: "since social reforms in the capitalist world are... an empty promise no matter what tactic one uses, the next logical step is necessarily disillusionment in social reform." People stopped trying to change society and left it to their politicians to do it for them. Small, evolutionary changes became the only possible alternative. In turn, parties like the SPD began to see revolutionary change as an obstacle to their own stability.

Luxemburg opposed reforms that blunt the class struggle not only because "they lose not only their supposed effectiveness, but also cease to be a means of preparing the working class for the proletarian conquest of power." In other words, the "struggle for reform is (the party's) *means*; the social revolution, its *goal*."

Reforms can improve living conditions or they can also build workers' confidence in self–organizing. The "difference is not in the what but in the how": whether a party grants reforms from the legislature or mobilizes people to fight for them. The former can be a means of social control, maintaining the smooth operation of accumulation and, by fixing some of capitalism's excesses, allowing a safety valve.

Bernstein's optimism and localism's pessimism are two sides of the same coin. Either "the 'means of adaptation' are really capable of stopping the breakdown of the capitalist system," as he believed, or they're capable of stopping people doing anything serious about it. Either way, "capitalism (can) maintain itself by suppressing its own contradictions." In the best–case scenario, left–wing officials suppress those contradictions; in the worst case, they get offloaded onto workers and the environment. The common assumption between Bernstein and Gibson–Graham is that capitalism is pervasive. We can embrace, tinker with or ignore it, but we can't end it. For theories based on building hope, this is a bleak prospect.

Even with its gradual reformism, the SPD still had a program for large–scale social change, something the localists have abandoned entirely. Today, as the market dominates more aspects of our lives, our democratic choices get narrower: we choose which of our ruling parties to elect, not whether they can make substantive change. But if neoliberalism weakens the prospects for reform, it also helps demonstrate the Marxist argument that capitalism can't create a humane world. The question then becomes: how do we spread that understanding, and how can people act on it?

Here's why movements for reform matter: not for their goals alone, which neoliberalism continually tries to restrict, but for the confidence and knowledge that they build. As Luxemburg suggests, the "great socialist significance of the trade–union and parliamentary struggles is that through them the *awareness*, the consciousness, of the proletariat becomes socialist, and it is organized as a class." Large, class–conscious workers' movements are only the beginning: they face "a long and stubborn struggle" with many defeats along the way. Local movements are key to this struggle when they challenge capitalist social relations, fighting for control over work processes, resources and against environmental degradation. Here are some examples of what local resistance *against* capitalism can look like. They're Canadian, but there are countless examples across the globe.

Participatory Budgeting in Toronto

With Participatory Budgeting (PB), people who are affected by a budget help to implement it. This is the best–case application of localism: it's a potentially radical democratic practice that gives marginalized people access to power at the local level. PB's most famous example is in the Brazilian city of Porto Alegre, after the Workers Party (PT) won city council elections in 1989. Previous city governments spent budgets almost entirely on wages and patronage deals. The PT government created a Participatory Budget, convening popular assemblies to channel funds into affordable housing, roadworks, water treatment and education. With concrete improvements came increased participation: from under 1000 citizens involved in 1990, over 20,000 were a part of the process by 2001. Many other cities adopted PB, including the entire state of Rio Grande do Sul from 1999 to 2002. But PB's legacy in Brazil has been mixed. Some reforms were made and different groups were brought into city politics. However, as PB grew, right–wing groups fought back, enforcing budget compromises that made it hard to redistribute income. After the PT implemented neoliberal measures, the party was defeated in the 2004 municipal elections, notably in Porto Alegre. The PT itself split, as radical leftists didn't want to be part of a neoliberal government. PB's radical, participatory model wasn't designed to deal with neoliberal opposition.

PB has been implemented in the Global North as well. The Toronto Community Housing Corporation (TCHC), with 164,000 tenants, is the second–biggest social housing corporation in North America and has implemented PB since 2001.[27] It grants $1.8 million dollars per year, or 13 percent of its annual $9 million capital projects budget, to a three–year process of tenant consultation and voting. Tenants make purchases like new hallway tiles, kitchen cupboards and gym facilities, learning democratic skills like public speaking along the way. The TCHC board must approve all decisions. Sacrifice is part of the process: not all tenants agree with the proposals, so participants learn to put the community's wellbeing over their own. According to its supporters, PB can reverse the decline of local democracy.

PB is a resolutely localist project. It promotes community values and activism and encourages democratic control over the market. But it's also a way to reconcile tenants to neoliberal policy. The TCHC management developed it in response to cutbacks in the 1990s. As one tenant said, "When you are sitting in your own community, you don't understand why they don't fix things or why you can't have the things you want.... With this budget process, people began to see how limited the funding was and the need for it out there." Rather than organizing to resist the cutbacks, the process framed them as inevitable. This is reinforced by the paltry amount PB allocates: the $1.8 million is a small part of the annual $138 million in capital costs, let alone the $564 million operating budget, and certainly a tiny amount compared to the $300 million backlog of needed repairs.

The Ontario Coalition Against Poverty (OCAP), a community organization that mobilizes poor people for direct, mass action, is also active in the TCHC. OCAP publicizes dilapidated TCHC properties, exposing management plans to sell them off when differential rents increase. The organization demands that TCHC conduct outstanding repairs and build new social housing to shrink the 10–year waiting list. It fights the targeting of non–status migrants in TCHC housing and power abuses by TCHC private security. Most importantly, OCAP frames all these actions politically, showing how the TCHC's deterioration and sell–offs are ways to enforce market rule. OCAP mobilizes tenants through mass meetings and occupations of building manager offices, confronting, rather than internalizing the neoliberal agenda.

PB advocates suggest many ways to get more people to participate. However, these are framed as technical, not political problems. In other words, it's okay to ask how budgeting works but not what the goals are. This makes sense: activists put in huge amounts of time to running and fine–tuning the process, and it's inevitable that perfecting the system, rather than changing its context, becomes a priority.

Worse, the budget limits of PB can demobilize the political capacities it develops. This is what happened in Porto Alegre when it rejected the PT municipal government after years of PB. It's no accident that the World Bank, in part responsible for designing the neoliberal agenda, is strongly pro–PB. In a classic, if unintended, reformist statement, an Austrian government report frames PB's ideological goals, calling it a "problem... that uninformed citizens may select policies that do not conform to the constraints placed on the government (i.e. participants vote to spend far more resources than are available)." Luckily, "most participants seem to be aware that PB programs overall impact will be limited by revenue and authority constraints placed on the government." Neoliberal administrators must implement capital's agenda for the "uninformed citizens." The "authority constraints" that maintain market rule are the questions that PB must never ask.

PB accepts the existing distribution of budget funds. OCAP's TCHC campaigns don't accept these limits, instead mobilizing tenants to confront poor conditions. And OCAP is more successful at getting funds than PB. At one apartment complex, OCAP demands led to $9 million of repairs, more than was allocated in four years of PB. OCAP is clear that local administrators work in favor of capital, not citizens and must be opposed.

The Special Diet Campaign

Mass resistance can start locally. In 1995, the Ontario Conservative government cut its already–meager welfare rates by 21.6 percent. At a time when monthly rent for a two–bedroom basement apartment cost $800 on average, a single mother of two received only $1,239 on welfare, leaving her and her kids just over $400 a month to live on.

The cuts were never restored. However, the legislation allowed recipients with health problems, like diabetes or heart disease, to claim up to $250 more for special diet needs. In 2005, as part of its Raise The Rates Campaign, OCAP began to mobilize welfare recipients to receive the special diet claim. OCAP organized a clinic at the provincial legislature, where supportive doctors assessed and approved over 1000 welfare recipients for the special diet. After this success, the group organized regular mass clinics. The Campaign highlighted poverty as the largest risk factor for poor health. The Campaign shifted millions of dollars from government accounts directly to poor people. From 2002 to 2007, OCAP increased the number of recipients from 5,300 to 31,000. It gave poor people more money for food, but it also helped create food security by freeing income for housing, transport and other needs.

The Campaign's success was repeated across the province, in much smaller towns like Belleville and Trenton, where hundreds of recipients were signed up. From a $2 million program in 2002, the special needs diet costs expanded to $25 million in 2005 and $200 million by 2010. In response the government tightened the rules, requiring doctors to specify recipients' health problems, violating patient privacy. The government and medical authorities pressured doctors to refuse to sign the forms. Welfare bureaucrats, not doctors, decided if a health condition was valid and individuals began to be targeted for fraud. The Toronto Sun newspaper helped by alleging claimants drove new SUVs or earned $65,000 per year. In Toronto, city officials refused to process claims from doctors still willing to submit them. The Minister for Community and Social Services admitted that living on welfare was unsafe but refused to lift the restrictions, blaming the public for not supporting "welfare abuse."

Despite provincial plans to cancel the Special Diet, the struggle continues, and OCAP has mobilized protests at municipal welfare offices in Toronto and built alliances with a union federation to protect it. What elevates the Special Diet Campaign above reform politics is OCAP's ability to build poor people's *political* capacities, since they've fought hard to keep the program. Rather than an act of charity, OCAP argues that unions should support the Special Diet because it's part of raising living standards for the whole working class and opposing cutbacks to the public service. The government's refusal to pay an extra $250 to poor people shows the true, anti–human face of neoliberalism, but it also shows just how effective the campaign has been. Raise the Rates is resolutely local: it addresses the living conditions of poor people directly, in communities across the province. However, it is not local*ist*: poor people aren't required to spend more time and energy trying to meet their basic needs. Instead, they're making demands on the state and targeting neoliberal policy.

Building counter–power: the Ontario Days of Action and the global Justice movement

Activist groups grow or shrink along with the movements themselves. But they have a special role to play as incubators of skills and political ideas, providing continuity between different struggles and becoming sites of counter–power for the broader left. Activists have built these poles of attraction across Canada many times: two examples include the Ontario Days of Action during the mid–1990s and the global justice movement of the late 1990s–early 2000s. The full story of these events has yet to be told, and this brief sketch won't do justice to the strategic issues these movements raise. However, they provide some lessons on how to organize at and beyond the local level.[28]

In response to the 1995 social services cutbacks, the Ontario Federation of Labor (OFL) and community group coalitions held one–day general strikes in cities across the province, culminating in the two–day Toronto strike on October 25–26, 1996 that shut down most public services, many private companies and brought 250,000 people onto the streets. Many activists felt the next logical step was a province–wide general strike. However, a group of private sector unions in the OFL made electing the social democratic New Democratic Party their top priority and pushed for a de–escalation, holding one–off Days of Actions in smaller cities again. By treating the mass movement as a spout, to be turned on and off when they needed it, the labor leadership squandered its momentum. The chance to create grassroots counter–power was lost.

The global justice movement went public at the November 1999 World Trade Organization (WTO) meetings in Seattle, where activists engaged in sit–down protests and snake marches, stealing the limelight and shutting down much of the event. A product of months of organizing by the largely anarchist Direct Action Network, the Seattle protests took the media by surprise and revitalized the anti–capitalist movement. They linked local issues like farm subsidies, pollution and labor rights to business and government agendas. The creativity and confrontation of anarchists and socialists gave hope to thousands of activists, who joined protests at other global meetings in Washington, Genoa and elsewhere.

Confronting and trying to shut down WTO public forums

gave activists a sense of collective power. This is because the movement wasn't just symbolic: it disrupted business–as–usual for the ruling class. Different movements started attending: for example, Green Party, NGO and trade union activists came together to protest the Summit of the Americas in Quebec City, on April 21–22, 2001. 5000 activists marched to the fence surrounding the conference in order to tear it down and confront attendees directly, while trade union leaders marched 20,000 members to a distant parking lot to hear 22 speeches. Radicals attempted to divert the larger crowd to protest at the fence, confronting official social movements that feared direct action and, more importantly, losing control over their members. Even in a protest led by reformists, political struggles gave radicals a chance to pose strategic questions about capitalist power and win people to militant tactics.

As the summit mobilizations grew, security forces became more aggressive, culminating in vicious attacks at the G8 summit at Genoa in July 2001, where police killed a protestor and beat and tortured detainees. More demonstrations took place in Washington DC in April 2002 and Kananaskis, Alberta in June 2002 and continue today. However, the World Trade Center attacks of September 2001 began to derail the movement, as mainstream labor leaders reaffirmed their patriotism and denounced direct action. The tentative links between radical and social democratic activists came undone.

What came to be known as summit–hopping was never going to bring down capitalism. But direct–action protest can link up to community and workplace struggles, building activist networks between high–profile events. In Ontario, the Rebuilding The Left initiative began in Toronto in 2000, as 700 activists from unions, social justice, socialist and community groups came together to build anti–capitalist political capacities. Initiatives also took place in Vancouver, Winnipeg and other cities. In 2000, OCAP started the Ontario Common Front, in which activists, trade unionists and community group members discussed how to build militant mass actions. In 2002, left–wing activists in the NDP asked similar questions, as they tried to form a left–wing bloc through the New Politics Initiative, before being defeated by the party leadership.

These movements didn't create long–term organizations of counter–power. Even the magnificent anti–Gulf War protests in 2003 didn't create long–term organizational gains. But efforts to build non–sectarian groups to confront capitalist power continue. On a much smaller scale, the Greater Toronto Workers Assembly initiative brings together different left–wing activist groups and individuals to create united anti–capitalist activism and fight governments' attempts to offload the economic crisis onto workers.

Making freedom global

This book has traced the roots of localism from classical political economy and its confusion over the source of value and abstract labor. These problems get reflected in both pro– and anti–market localist schemes for ethical small business and alternative economies, which can't defeat capitalism's drive to achieve SNALT. Similarly, capital centralization and rent limit the prospects for urban agriculture. The idea that small–scale alternatives can change the world, despite the evidence to the contrary, comes from the petite bourgeois whose attempt to rise through their own efforts leads to a host of moralistic solutions. Localism mobilizes the values of solidarity for neoliberalism, letting governments download services onto poor communities. It has encouraged illusions in the potential of social, micro–enterprise to undercut large firms. As Luxemburg recognized, it's not possible "to construct an unbroken chain of continually growing reforms leading from the present social order to socialism." It's still less likely for those reforms to lead to localism, since it refutes large–scale social reforms in the first place. Through all these criticisms, this book has tried to show that small–scale alternatives are only viable when they occupy niches of the capitalist marketplace. They can't provide a lasting basis for building a noncapitalist society, because capital by its nature doesn't tolerate competitors for long.

But that doesn't mean we have to accept that limited, small–scale survival strategies are all that's possible. Grassroots mass anti–capitalist struggles created trade unions, the welfare state, anti–colonial movements and dozens of revolutionary moments that prefigured a new, non–exploitative society. We can at least consider Luxemburg's boast that "there can be no socialism outside of Marxist socialism," not because Marxism is ethically superior to localism or utopianism, but because it's a *criticism of capitalism*, showing how its contradictory laws of motion mobilize people to end them.

In a society that takes away the means to survive outside the market, and offers either unemployment or tedious work as a reward, workers have every right to survive however they can. For many people, this means scavenging, growing food or setting up a cooperative, and we should celebrate their sheer tenacity. But surely the more important question is: how do we change society so people can flourish, not just survive? If a postcapitalist society is filled with happy, cooperative gardeners, and if after the revolution Burning Man permanently fills the Nevada Desert, so be it. As Marx famously described communism in *The German Ideology*, he could "hunt in the morning, fish in the afternoon, rear cattle in the evening and criticize after dinner" without being defined as a hunter, fisher, farmer or critic. A postcapitalist utopia might equally be filled with billions of people expressing their full humanity through networked, motion–sensing gaming consoles. The use–values that promote community and solidarity are as individual as the people using them and will become more so, once our individuality is freed from the confines of wage–labor.

The localist future isn't a bad place to be. But understanding how we get there imposes some heavy, capitalocentric restrictions: how capital must expand and centralize at any cost, and how the system must ultimately be ended if that process is to stop. The people who resist need social movements that build their political capacities. The social anarchist Bookchin, describing Libertarian Municipalism, calls for "the development of serious organizations, a radical politics, a committed social movement, theoretical coherence, and programmatic relevance." As part of the struggle to gain power, activists create political counter–institutions to deal directly with community problems. This is a first, and only the first, step on the road to dual power. It's very different from Solidarity Economic's internalization of market priorities, or Parecon's post–revolutionary schemes that don't provide political tools to achieve them. These linkages show how socialists and some localists can find common ground in anti–capitalist struggle.

Luxemburg warns that "the chain breaks quickly, and the paths that the movement can take from that point are many and varied." Political organization helps shape how struggle turns out. This doesn't mean waiting for a revolutionary socialist party, although it could mean creating groups that can contribute to a future one. Those groups can help "recognize the direction of (capitalist) development and then, in the political struggle, push its consequences to the extreme." Capitalism's social contradictions must be revealed and resisted. Localism, when it relies on neoclassical ideas and refuses to oppose capitalism, doesn't help. But there's nothing anti–local about socialism. We can confront global institutions of capitalist power in local spaces: when anti–capitalists take on local and community struggles, they're educating themselves and others about how to resist capitalism on the ground. The campaigns briefly sketched above have made demands that build political capacities and show how capital can't meet human needs at any scale. There are hundreds of others around the world to be created and built: in a time of economic crisis and revolutionary awakening, these tasks take on some urgency. The fight for reforms must have a revolutionary strategy at its heart, confronting the capitalist social relations that localism refuses to.

Notes and References

1   This book draws on many localist sources, including: Bellows and Hamm 2001; Berry 1996; Carrlson 2008; Daly 1996; Daly and Farley 2004; Estill 2008; Kingsolver 2007; McKibben 2007; McRobie 1981; Morris 1996; Petrini 1007; Roberts 2001; Roberts 2008; Schumacher 1999; Shuman 2007; Smith and MacKinnon 2007

2   Howard and King 1985, pp. 65–133; Hunt 2002, pp. 100–102, 283–313

3   Marx 1977, *Capital Volume One* provides the theoretical underpinning for many of these arguments. See excerpts from Chapter One on commodities, pp. 134–170; Chapter 15 on machines, pp. 492–639; Chapter 24 on surplus value, pp. 728–730; and Chapters 31 and 32 on the birth of industrial capitalism; Ciccantell and Smith 2009, pp. 363–379

4   Marx 1973 B, pp. 47–67; Proudhon 1972, p. 285; Proudhon 1966, pp. 124–286; Therborn 1976, pp. 79–109

5   Albo 2009; Marx 1981, pp. 195–196, 1056

6   Bookchin 1995, pp. 34–35, 48–51; Harvey 2006, pp. 42, 80–91, 247, 381; Ingham 2004, pp. 184–187; McNally 1993, pp. 34, 76, 137–158; Meeker–Lowry 1996, pp. 449–458

7   Biehl and Bookchin 1998, pp. 61–97; Mandel 1977, pp. 310–325, 503–521

8   Food and Hunger Action Committee 2001, pp. 8–42; Toronto Food Policy Council 1999, pp. 1–20

9   Mandel 1968, pp. 279–295, 365; Key and Roberts 2007. See Woodhouse 2010 on how difficult it is to quantify the benefits of small farms.

10   This discussion of rent draws on Fine 1979; Marx 1981; Murray 1977; Murray 1978; O'Connor 1973

11   Friendly 2008, pp. 7–50; Kirkpatrick and Tarasuk 2009, pp. 135–138

12 Levins 2005, pp. 21–22; Gropas 2006, pp. 253–265

13 Engels 1970; Katz 1986, p. 72–76

14 Orwell 1977, pp. 86–90, 142–160

15 Therborn 1979, p. 121; Wright 1997, pp. 72–77; Bourdieu 1984, pp. 177–179, 333–371

16 Draper 1989, pp. 3, 10–20; Engels 1970

17 Williams 1980, pp. 203–212; Hahnel 2005, pp. 60–63, 268–376

18 Eagleton 2007, pp. 114–120; Gramsci 1971, pp. 5–11, 210–238

19 For the relation between localism and neoliberalism see: Amin 2005, pp. 613–630; Albo 1996, pp. 2–39; Gough 2002, p. 407–421; Jessop 2002, pp. 463–467; Zuege 2000, pp. 90–105

20 Gibson–Graham 2002, pp. 4–14; Gibson–Graham 2006, pp. 59–76; Miller A; Miller B; Stolarski; Community Economies Collective 2001, p. 2

21 Preobrazhensky 1965, pp. 218–219

22 Camfield 2007, pp. 2–4

23 Holloway 2005 A, pp. 121–126; Holloway 2005 B, p. 274; Shaikh 1978, pp. 220–236; Luxemburg 1971, pp. 62–64, 119–127; Albert and Hahnel 2004, pp. 193, 259

24 Holloway's criticism rests on Lenin's famous 1902 polemic, *What Is To Be Done?*, in which an educated revolutionary elite enlightens the masses. But this tactic was never meant to be permanent: the Bolsheviks were addressing the extremely repressive conditions of the Tsarist dictatorship, which imposed a few of its own hierarchies on its opponents like exile, jail and execution. The February 1917 revolution created formal democracy in Russia; Lenin, seeing that the conditions were ripe for mass revolution, called on the Russian working class to remake democracy from below through workers' councils. These flourished and provided the backbone of the October Revolution, until they were crushed under the weight of the devastating Russian Civil War. There's no direct line from Marx to Stalin, and reading the crimes of the USSR back onto capitalist laws of motion is

judging by hindsight. That history had many possible outcomes.

25 Lenin 1960, pp. 58, 595–598. See also: Ahmad 1992; Anderson 2002; Eagleton 2007; Trotsky 1969, Chapter 7

26 Marx 1973 A, p. 405

27 Bruce 2004; Lerner 2006; Wampler 2000; http://www.toronto-housing.ca/; for OCAP's activism, see their website, http://www.ocap.ca/

28 See the *New Socialist* magazine archive at: http://www.newsocialist.org/

Bibliography

How green are small businesses? A snapshot of environmental awareness and practice in small and medium sized enterprises (SMEs). (2002) Bristol: Environment Agency

Food and Hunger Action Committee Phase II Report. (2001) Food and Hunger Action Committee

Ahmad, Aijaz (1992) *In Theory: Classes, Nations, Literature.* London: Verso

Albert, M and Hahnel, R (2004) *Parecon: life after capitalism.* New York: Verso

Albo, G.(2007) "Neoliberalism and the Discontented." In (eds) L. Panitch & C. Leys *Socialist Register 2008: Global Flashpoints.* (pp 354–362). London: Merlin Press

——. 17 September 2009, *Personal Communication,* Toronto

——. "The Limits of Eco–Localism: Scale, Strategy, Socialism." In (eds) L. Panitch & C. Leys *Socialist Register 2007: Coming to Terms with Nature.* Eds. (pp 337–364). London: Merlin Press

(1996) A World Market of Opportunities? Capitalist Obstacles and Left Economic Policy. In (eds) L. Panitch & C. Leys *Socialist Register 1997: Ruthless Criticism of All That Is* (pp 5–47). London: Merlin Press

Albritton, R (2009) *Let Them Eat Junk: How Capitalism Creates Hunger and Obesity.* Winnipeg: Arbeiter Ring

Anderson, K B (2002) Marx's late writings on non–Western and precapitalist societies and gender. *Rethinking Marxism,* 14, 4:84–96

Bellows, A C and Hamm, M W (2001) Local autonomy and sustainable development: Testing import substitution in local-izing food systems. *Agriculture and Human Values,* 18271–284

Berry, W (1996) Conserving Communities. In (eds) J. Mander & E. Goldsmith *The Case Against The Global Economy, and For A Turn Toward the Local* San Francisco: Sierra Club Books

Biehl, J and Bookchin, M (1998) *The politics of social ecology: libertarian municipalism.* Montreal: Black Rose Books

Bookchin, M (1995) *Social anarchism or lifestyle anarchism: the unbridgeable chasm.* San Francisco: AK Press

Bourdieu, P (1984) *Distinction: a social critique of the judgement of taste.* London: Routledge and Kegan Paul

Bruce, I (2004) *The Porto Alegre Alternative: Direct Democracy in Action.* London: Pluto Press

Camfield, D. (2007) *On "Postmodern Marxism" and its Class Theory.* Unpublished.

Carrlson, C (2008) *Nowtopia: how pirate programmers, outlaw bicyclists, and vacant–lot gardeners are inventing the future today.* Oakland: AK Press

Ciccantell, P and Smith, D A (2009) Rethinking Global Commodity Chains: Integrating Extraction, Transport, and Manufacturing. *International Journal of Comparative Sociology,* 50, 3–4:361–384

Community Economies Collective (2001) Imagining and Enacting Noncapitalist Futures. *Socialist Review,* 28, 3–4:93–135

Cunningham, M and Houston, D (2004) *The Andersonville Study of Retail Economics.* Chicago: Civic Economics

Dachner, N (2008) *Personal Communication*, University of Toronto Dalla Lana School of Public Health, Toronto

Daly, H E and Farley, J (2004) *Ecological economics: principles and applications.* Washington: Island Press

Draper, H (1989) *Karl Marx's Theory of Revolution Volume Four: Critique of Other Socialisms.* 1989:Monthly Review Press

Draper, H (1966) The Two Souls of Socialism. *New Politics,* 5, 1:57–84

Eagleton, T (2007) *Ideology: An Introduction.* London: Verso

Engels, F (1970) *The Housing Question.* Moscow: Progress Publishers

Engels, F (1970) Socialism: Utopian and Scientific. In *Marx/Engels Selected Works, Volume 3* (pp 95–151). Moscow: Progress

Publishers

Estill, L (2008) *Small is possible: Life in a local economy.* Gabriola Island: New Society Publishers

Fine, B (1979) On Marx's theory of agricultural rent. *Economy and Society,* 8, 3:241–278

Foster, J B (2000) *Marx's Ecology.* New York: Monthly Review Press

Friendly, A (2008) *Towards Food Security Policy for Canada's Social Housing Sector.* Ottawa: Canadian Policy Research Networks Inc. and Social Housing Services Corporation

Gibson–Graham, J K (2006) Imagining and Enacting a Postcapitalist Feminist Economic Politics. *Women's Studies Quarterly,* 34, 1–2:72–78

Gibson–Graham, J K (2002) Beyond Global vs. Local: Economic Politics Outside the Binary Frame. In (eds) A. Herod & M.W. Wright *Geographies of Power: Placing Scale* Malden: Blackwell Publishers

Gough, J (2002) Neoliberalism and Socialisation in the Contemporary City: Opposites, Complements and Instabilities. *Antipode,* 34, 3:405–426

Gramsci, A (1971) The Modern Prince. In (eds) Q. Hoare & G.N. Smith *Selections from the prison notebooks of Antonio Gramsci* New York: International Publishers

Gropas, M (2006) Landscape, revolution and property regimes in rural Havana. *Journal of Peasant Studies,* 33, 2:248–277

Grow the Greenbelt: Protect Markham's Foodbelt and Quality of Life, Stop Sprawl. (n.date), Accessed 25 January 2010

Hahnel, R (2007) Eco–localism: A Constructive Critique. *Capitalism Nature Socialism,* 18, 2:62–78

Hahnel, R (2005) *Economic justice and democracy: from competition to cooperation.* New York: Routledge

Harvey, D (2006) *The Limits To Capital.* London: Verso

Holloway, J (2005) *Change the World Without Taking Power.* London: Pluto Press

Holloway, J (2005) No. *Historical Materialism,* 13, 4:265–284

Howard, M C and King, J E (1985) *The Political Economy of Marx.* Second edn, New York: New York University Press

Hseih, L H T (2010) Markham's farmers denounce foodbelt. *Yorkregion.com* 14 January 2010, Accessed 16 February 2010

Hunt, EK (2002) *History of economic thought: a critical perspective.* Second Edition. Armonk, N.Y.: M.E. Sharpe

Jessop, B (2002) Liberalism, Neoliberalism, and Urban Governance: A State–Theoretical Perspective. *Antipode,* 34, 3:452–472

Katz, S (1986) Towards a Sociological Definition of Rent: Notes on David Harvey's *The Limits to Capital. Antipode,* 8, 1:64–78

Key Small Business Statistics. (2010) Ottawa: Industry Canada

Key, N and Roberts, M J (2007) *Measures of Trends in Farm size Tell Differing Stories* in *Amber Waves: The Economics of Food, Farming, Natural Resources and Rural America .*U.S. Department of Agriculture

Kingsolver, B (2007) *Animal, vegetable, miracle: a year of food life.* New York: HarperCollins Publishers

Kirkpatrick, S and Tarasuk, V (2009) Food insecurity and participation in community food programs among low–income Toronto families. *Canadian Journal of Public Health,* 100, 2:135–139

Kovel, J (2007) *The enemy of nature: the end of capitalism or the end of the world?* Second edn, New York: Zed Books

Lenin, V I (1960) The Development of Capitalism in Russia. In *Collected Works, Volume 3*Moscow: Progress Publishers

Lenin, V I (1943) The Dual Power. In *Selected Works, Volume VI* (pp 27–30). New York: International Publishers Co., Inc.

Lerner, J. 2006, *Let The People Decide: Transformative Community Development Through Participatory Budgeting in Canada*

Levins, R (2005) How Cuba is Going Ecological. *Capitalism, Nature, Socialism,* 16, 3:7–27

Luxemburg, R (1971) Social Reform or Revolution. In (ed) D.

Howard *Selected Political Writings* (pp 52–134). New York: Monthly Review

Luxemburg, R (1915) *The Junius Pamphlet*. Marxists Internet Archive. Web. 01 April 2009.

Malthus, T R (1970) *An essay on the principle of population; and, A summary view of the principle of population.* Harmondsworth: Penguin

Mandel, E (1977) *Late Capitalism.* London: New Left Books

Mandel, E (1968) *Marxist Economic Theory.* New York: Monthly Review Press

Marx, K (1981) *Capital: A Critique of Political Economy.* London: Penguin Books

Marx, K (1977) *Capital: A Critique of Political Economy.* New York: Vintage Books

Marx, K (1973 A) The Eighteenth Brumaire of Louis–Napoleon. In *Karl Marx and Frederick Engels: Selected Works in three volumes, Volume One* (pp 394–487). Moscow: Progress Publishers

Marx, K (1973 B) *The Poverty of Philosophy.* Moscow: Progress Publishers

Marx, K and Engels, F (1998) *The Communist Manifesto: A Modern Edition.* London: Verso

Luxemburg, R (1915) *The Junius Pamphlet*. [online] Marxists Internet Archive. Available from http://www.marxists.org /archive/luxemburg/1915/junius/index.htm (Accessed 25 March 2010)

McKibben, W (2007) *Deep economy: the wealth of communities and the durable future.* New York: Times Books

McNally, D (1993) *Against the Market: Political Economy, Market Socialism and the Marxist Critique.* London: Verso

McRobie, G (1981) *Small is Possible.* New York: Harper and Row

Meeker–Lowry, S (1996) Community Money: The Potential of *Local* Currency. In (eds) J. Mander & E. Goldsmith *The Case Against The Global Economy, and For A Turn Toward the Local*

San Francisco: Sierra Club Books

Miller, E (n.date) *Other Economies Are Possible: Building a Solidarity Economy* Grassroots Economic Organizing. (Accessed 12 April 2008)

Miller, E (n.date) *Our Eyes On the Prize: From a 'Worker Co–op Movement' to a Transformative Social Movement* Grassroots Economic Organizing. (Accessed 24 March 2008)

Morris, D (1996) Communities: Building Authority, Responsibility, and Capacity. In (eds) J. Mander & E. Goldsmith *The Case Against The Global Economy, and For A Turn Toward the Local* San Francisco: Sierra Club Books

Murray, R (1978) Value and Theory of Rent: Part Two. *Capital and Class,* Spring, 4:11–33

Murray, R (1977) Value and Theory of Rent: Part One. *Capital and Class,* Autumn, 3:100–122

O'Connor, J (1973) *The Fiscal Crisis of the State.* New York: St. Martin's Press, Inc.

Orwell, G (1977) *The road to Wigan Pier.* Harmondsworth: Penguin Press

Pelletier, N, Tyedmers, P and Sonesson, U (2009) Not All Salmon Are Created Equal: Life Cycle Assessment (LCA) of Global Salmon Farming Systems. *Environmental Science and Technology,* 43, 23:8730–8736

Petrini, C (2007) *Slow Food Nation: Why Our Food Should Be Good, Clean and Fair.* New York: Rissoli Ex Libris

Preobrazhensky, E A (1965) *The New Economics.* Oxford: Oxford University Press

Proudhon, P (1972) *General Idea of the Revolution in the Nineteenth Century.* New York: Gordon Press

Proudhon, P (1966) *What is Property? An Inquiry into the Principle of Right and of Government.* New York: H. Fertig

Roberts, W (2008) *The No–Nonsense Guide to World Food.* Toronto: New Internationalist Publications Ltd

Roberts, W (2001) *The Way to a City's Heart is Through its Stomach.*

Toronto: Toronto Food Policy Council

Saad Filho, A (2004) Towards a Pro–poor Development Strategy for Middle–Income Countries: A Comment on Bresser–Pereira and Nakano. *Brazilian Journal of Political Economy*, 24, 1:130–135

Sargeant, W and Moutray, C (2010) *The Small Business Economy: A Report to the President*. Washington, DC: US Small Business Administration (SBA) Office of Advocacy

Schumacher, E F (1999) *Small is Beautiful: Economics as if People Mattered. 25 Years later... with commentaries*. Vancouver: Hartley & Marks Publishers Inc.

Shaikh, A (1978) An Introduction to the History of Crisis Theories. In *U.S. Capitalism in Crisis* New York: Union of Radical Political Economists

Shuman, M (2007) *The Small–Mart revolution: how local businesses are beating the global competition*. San Francisco: Berrett–Koehler Publishers, Inc.

Smith, A and MacKinnon, J (2007) *The 100 Mile Diet*. Toronto: Random House Canada

Stolarski, L (n.date) *A Strategy for Unions and Coops: Toward Building A Labor–Ownership Economy* Grassroots Economic Organizing.

Therborn, G (1979) *What does the ruling class do when it rules?* London: Verso

Therborn, G (1976) *Science, Class and Society: On the Formation of Sociology and Historical Materialism*. London: NLB

Wampler, B (2000) *A Guide to Participatory Budgeting. Participation and Sustainable Development in Europe*. n. pub.: Austrian Ministry of the Environment

Weber, C L and Matthews, H S (2008) Food–miles and the relative climate impacts of food choices in the United States. *Environmental Science and Technology*, 42, 10:3508–3513

Whitford, D (2009) Can Farming Save Detroit? *Cnn.com* 29 December 2009, Accessed 17 February 2010

Williams, R (1980) Base and Superstructure in Marxist Cultural Theory. In *Problems in Materialism and Culture* (pp 31–49). London: Verso

Williams, R (1980) Utopia and Science Fiction. In *Problems in Materialism and Culture: Selected Essays* (pp 196–212). London: Verso

Woodhouse, P (2010) "Beyond Industrial Agriculture? Some Questions about Farm Size, Productivity and Sustainability." *Journal of Agrarian Change,* 10,3: 437–453

Wright, E O (1997) *Class Counts.* Cambridge: Cambridge University Press

Zuege, A (2000) The Chimera of the Third Way. In (eds) L. Panitch & C. Leys *Socialist Register 2000: Necessary and Unnecessary Utopias* Blackpoint: Fernwood Press

Contemporary culture has eliminated both the concept of the public and the figure of the intellectual. Former public spaces – both physical and cultural – are now either derelict or colonized by advertising. A cretinous anti-intellectualism presides, cheerled by expensively educated hacks in the pay of multinational corporations who reassure their bored readers that there is no need to rouse themselves from their interpassive stupor. The informal censorship internalized and propagated by the cultural workers of late capitalism generates a banal conformity that the propaganda chiefs of Stalinism could only ever have dreamt of imposing. Zer0 Books knows that another kind of discourse – intellectual without being academic, popular without being populist – is not only possible: it is already flourishing, in the regions beyond the striplit malls of so-called mass media and the neurotically bureaucratic halls of the academy. Zer0 is committed to the idea of publishing as a making public of the intellectual. It is convinced that in the unthinking, blandly consensual culture in which we live, critical and engaged theoretical reflection is more important than ever before.

Printed and bound by CPI Group (UK) Ltd, Croydon, CR0 4YY